The Living Water

Refreshing Your Soul

Dear Kevin & Jena,
Thank you for using
y'all's gift to bless me
and many others!

~Jim
1 Cor. 12:7

James A. Solomon

outskirtspress
DENVER, COLORADO

The Living Water
Refreshing Your Soul
All Rights Reserved.
Copyright © 2014 James A. Solomon
v2.0

Outskirts Press, Inc.
http://www.outskirtspress.com

ISBN: 978-1-4327-8018-0

Outskirts Press and the "OP" logo are trademarks belonging to Outskirts Press, Inc.

PRINTED IN THE UNITED STATES OF AMERICA

TABLE OF CONTENTS

DEDICATION

This book is dedicated to the Author of Life, Our Lord and Savior Jesus Christ, and His next best gift to me after Himself, Anne, my wife, and our wonderful "princesses," Amanda and Ashley.

INTRODUCTION

I will never forget going hiking with my older daughter, Amanda, in the Lower Pagausset State Forest towards the end of Amanda's second year of life. I wondered if she'd ever see the third! We started off on a marked trail and soon found out that the trails we ended upon were not marked at all. Not only that, but we couldn't even "back-track," as everything began to look the same. We had packed only enough water and "animal crackers" to last until lunchtime when we had planned to return home. By the time we tried every path possible, with Amanda falling asleep in my arms after saying "Daddy, I'm tired, hungry, and thirsty" (which made me feel even worse than I already did regarding how "neglectful" I unintentionally had been), it was 3:00 in the afternoon!

I panicked. I wondered where all the other hikers were, even though most people worked on Monday-my day off! I began to pray, not only for God to give me strength to continue on until someone found us or we found them, but also for God to give me trust that He would somehow rescue me from the trap I had set for myself (at least for Amanda's sake). I prayed and prayed. I looked around: no other hikers. I looked down: nowhere to safely rest. I looked up: no helicopters or rescue planes in sight! Finally, I cried, begging God to allow Anne (my wife) and Ashley, my other daughter, to have more time on earth with me and Amanda, as they didn't seem to be ready to say "goodbye" just yet. It seemed as if, at the very moment

I gave up all hope in finding my way out of the wilderness by my own efforts, the Lord provided a way out of it through my reliance, not on myself but on Him.

At the end of another dirt "road to nowhere," a young woman drove up in a small car. In the back seat was her two-year-old son. She informed me that I was about 11 miles away from where I began! She offered a ride, and I didn't even hesitate to say yes, even in a day when "paranoia" was well founded. With Amanda cuddled up on my lap, as I sat in the passenger seat (realizing this was illegal in the state of Connecticut), I asked Tabatha, our driver, if she knew Jesus. She responded, "Why do you ask?" To which I responded, "Because you are an answer to my prayers to Him." Halfway back to our car, Amanda woke up, looked up, and asked, "Daddy, Who is *that* (looking at Tabatha)?" I told Amanda that Tabatha was an angel. Just as Amanda started looking for Tabatha's wings, we arrived at our car.

Still somewhat traumatized, hopefully without Amanda realizing it, I asked Amanda where she would like to go to eat before we went home. We had a wonderful time at McDonald's-so much so that Amanda seemed to only talk about that time eating out together when later asked by her mother what she did with daddy all day.

More time passed. Anne asked Amanda if she'd like to go on a hike with daddy again. Amanda responded, "We never found the water!" Anne didn't know what Amanda was talking about. Yet, later that day, when Anne told me about her conversation with Amanda, I realized what God was saying to me through her!

I took Amanda's statement to mean that she, with an unbelievably strong memory for a child her age, somehow remembered that we had set off on our journey together to find waterfalls that I had once seen with a friend (who knew where *he* was going!). But something hit home that evening. I realized that the Lord gave me a tiny glimpse of what it might have been like years ago for the Israelites who wandered through the wilderness for forty years before finally entering into the Promised Land. They strived and strived. Yet, because of their spiritual blindness, they never found the water, the Living Water that is, promised to them from God.

We too, even in the midst of doing things for the Lord, often lose sight of Him in the process. When we do so, we are completely blind, wandering aimlessly, lost in the wilderness of this world and the lost-ness of our lives, never finding that water that can quench our thirst forever.

It is my prayer and hope that the Lord will use the pages of this book to quench your soul's thirst for *Him*. In a dry and weary land, may the pages of this book give to you the rich and wonderful hope that is ours as we draw closer to the One whose well never runs dry.

THE BOOK OF ALL BOOKS

A Devotional based on Luke 1:1-4

There Are Many Good Books In The World, Right? Maybe. But the Bible is *certainly* set apart from the rest. That is why Luke could say that he wrote his account of the Good News so that we could know the *certainty* of the things we have been taught (Luke 1:4).

Several years ago I had a conversation with a friend, "Chris," who I met in Boston. A Yale graduate, and a successful businessman, Chris was the type of person who knew how to think before he spoke. It was that weekend that I openly shared my faith in Christ and His Word, known as the Bible, with Dawn, Chris' sister-in-law and life-time friend of mine, for the first time. His response: "There are many good books in the world-the bible is just one of them." This intelligent, ivy-league graduate seemed unable to rest until he made that statement.

Although there are many points that could be made in regard to the validity and trustworthiness of the Bible (from historical evidence, archeological finds, scholarly internal/external evidence tests, and most of all, changed lives), I'd like to point out only one: fulfilled prophecy. Any earnest seeker with an open mind will find that there are literally hundreds of prophetic words of the Old Testament fulfilled over time and recorded in the New Testament (i.e., Isaiah 52:13 through 53:12 is the most quoted passage from the Old Testament in the New

1

Testament). As Josh McDowell tells us, those who insist on facts rather than faith will find that "The evidence demands a verdict."

Move over psychic astrologers and tarot card readers! Move over Nostradamus and anybody else with foggy fore-telling of the future! When it comes to predicting the future, God's Word is like no other, as it is without error and without fallacy. Also, it is given for our own good, rather than the gain of the person making predictions (i.e., the book of Jonah; 2 Peter 1:20-21; 2 Timothy 3:16-17, etc.). It is even given without selfish financial gain (1 Timothy 6:10). There are no "$9.99 per minute" charges! As we read in the Old Testament book of Deuteronomy, if what a prophet proclaims does not take place or come true (accurately, at that), then that prophet has spoken presumptuously. We don't have to be concerned about what he/she has proclaimed (Deut. 18:22). Neither should we pay them for their advice.

One morning, the New York Times "quote of the day," from Senator Tom Daschle, then senate majority leader, in re-gard to President Bush's policy for the "war on terrorism," read as follows: "I don't think it would do anybody any good to second-guess what has been done to date. I think it has been successful. I've said that on many, many occasions. But I think the jury's still out about future success."

The jury is indeed still out about the future-this world's future, our nation's future, and your future. Yet, there is only One Judge who knows the verdict in advance. He predicted it to us when He said in His Word, "Here I am! I stand at the door and knock. If anyone hears my voice and opens the door, I will come in and eat with that person, and that person with me. To the one who overcomes, I will give the right to sit with me on my throne, just as I have overcome and sat down with my Father on his throne (Revelation 3:20-21)." Regarding those who *let him in*, he says, "I will wipe away every tear from their eyes. There will be no more death or mourning or crying or pain, for the old order of things has passed away (Revelation 21:4)."

Have the old order of things in *your life* passed away? If not, why not? We can never become secure in our lives, or even our eternal destiny, without knowing the One (John 14:6) who holds the future, regardless of what the future holds. Will *you* open the door to your future with him? If not, then you are keeping it closed intentionally, and His door will one day be closed permanently. Until then, we are given the choice to live not only by facts, but by faith, in the Author of faith Himself, our Lord Jesus Christ. To Him be the glory!

THE PATH OF LIFE

A Devotional based on Genesis 36:1-37:1

In the world of their day, Esau was a man of influence while Jacob may have been seen as a man of insignificance. Esau's kingdom was one of human will. Jacob's kingdom was one of heavenly wisdom. Esau belonged to a kingdom of self-reliance. Jacob belonged to a kingdom of self-denial. Esau's kingdom depended upon the power of men. Jacob's kingdom depended upon the promise of God. Esau's kingdom was one of "instant gratification." Jacob's kingdom was one of long-awaited joy. Esau belonged to a kingdom that was temporal, whereas Jacob belonged to a kingdom that is eternal. Many kings descended from Esau's line. The King of kings descended from Jacob's.

The promised Messiah (Isaiah 7:14, 9:2,6,7), the Savior of the World (Matthew 1:21), the Lord of the Universe (Colossians 1:16,17), Jesus the Christ (Luke 2:1-20), came in the "wrong" form when he was first presented in a stable, lying in a manger used to feed animals, to an economically disadvantaged couple from a town of no worldy renknown. In the eyes of most people of the day, the Messiah was not supposed to come that way. A king is normally seated on a throne in a palace rather than a manger in a stable. Yet, the Messiah was not born in a palace or to a family of influence.

God seldom does things the way people expect. And God uses unlikely characters to get His work done. Who would have thought that Jacob's family line would lead to Christ, or that all of history would pivot on Mary's baby, born in Bethlehem?

The Apostle Paul wrote to the church at Corinth that God does extraordinary things through ordinary people. Not many high born or powerful people were in that church. But God was using the "weak" people to shake a pagan city made up of people who thought they were "strong."

Consequently, most people miss the visitation of God, as we are more concerned about building our own "kingdom" rather than receiving admittance into His kingdom. They did then and we do today. The real tragedy is that the people of God also miss the motions of God's grace. We, too, look in the wrong places, expecting God to do things our way. As a result, just as Jesus said of Jerusalem, we do not recognize the time of God's visitation (Luke 19:44). We also do not follow in His footsteps, the steps of One who used all of the authority in the universe, to which He had a right, to serve, rather than to be served, and to give His life as a ransom for many (Matthew 20:28).

We have a choice. We can either travel down the road most traveled, the road of pride and arrogance, self-reliance and worldly influence, or the road less traveled, the road of humility and honesty, selfless love and Godly dependence. The choices we make will determine the kingdom in which we belong. Will that be a kingdom of this world, a kingdom that will one day end, or the Kingdom of Christ, a kingdom that will never end?

YOU'VE GOT MAIL

Getting Ready

A Devotional based on the Book of Revelation

*"Blessed is the one who reads the words of this prophecy,
and blessed are those who hear it and take to heart
what is written in it, because the time is near."*

Revelation 1:3

A trumpet sound. Seven golden lampstands. Eyes like blazing fire. Feet like bronze glowing in a furnace. A voice like the sound of rushing waters. Seven stars. A sharp double-edged sword coming out of a mouth. A face like the sun. A scroll. Seals. Four living creatures. Horses. A dragon. A beast of the Sea. A beast of the earth. A river. The Lamb.

Even the great reformer, John Calvin, admitted his uncertainty about what to do with the book of Revelation. Even though he completed volumes of commentaries on almost all of the rest of the New Testament, Calvin didn't write a commentary on the book of Revelation. Interpreters throughout history have shared Calvin's perplexity. Some would even say that many writers of popular commentaries and guides to its prophecies today might have done better to follow in Calvin's steps! Yet, still, we are called to try to make sense of it all, so that we can not only "hear" it but also take it "to heart," as we read above.

Revelation has highly symbolic and figurative imagery that we dare not interpret too literally. If so, we will be more concerned with identifying the woman dressed in purple and scarlet, the beast out of the sea, and the enormous red dragon with seven heads and ten horns than we would be about identifying what is keeping us from being prepared to meet our Lord face to face. It is important to determine the symbolic elements of Revelation and what they stand for. Yet, it is even more important to determine where we are in our hearts and minds in regard to our relationship with Christ verses where we need to be should He return today.

The "mail" that the seven churches in Revelation received then and there (chapters 2-3) contains the messages that we must receive here and now. Let's discover those messages in order to be best prepared for the Messenger through Whose Word we discover true life.

When Jesus said "Do not be afraid. I am the First and the Last. I am the Living One; I was dead, and behold I am alive forever and ever! And I hold the keys of death and Hades (Rev. 1:17b-18)," He reminded John, as He reminds us, that if we know Him, we have "nothing to fear but fear itself."

Yet, we must ask, how *well* do we know Him? Do we merely know *about* Him, or do we truly *know* Him? If you are not growing in knowing Him and making Him known, you are probably forsaking your true "first love (Rev. 2:4)." Do not wait until it is too late! If we let the Lord be our light (John 1:4), we won't be left in the dark, without a lampstand (Rev. 2:5), but instead can walk in the light, with our Lord.

DO OR DIE

*"Do not be afraid of what you are about to suffer.
I tell you, the devil will put some of you in prison
to test you...Be faithful, even to the point of
death, and I will give you the crown of life."*

Revelation 2:10-11

At the beginning of the message to the believers in Smyrna, the Lord describes Himself as the One who is the "First and the Last, who *died* and *came to life again* (vs. 8)." How significant a description, considering that these believers were to suffer tremendously, staring death in the face, because of their faith. Correspondingly, at the end of His message to the believers in Smyrna, Christ Jesus promises these same believers that they will never experience the "second death (vs. 11)."

During our seminary years in California, my wife and I once saw a bumper sticker stating the following: "Born once, die twice. Born twice, die once." Although we don't particularly care for bumper stickers, we liked this one, as it said in a succinct way what we all need to remember: When we are born not only physically, but born again, spiritually (John 3:3), it is true that we will one day die only physically and not spiritually (John 3:36). In other words, we "will not be hurt at all by the second death (2:11)." If we not only know Christ as our Savior but also follow Him as our Lord, never compromising our convictions despite the costs of our calling (Matthew 5:11), we will be able to move forward in faith rather than fear (2:10a). Likewise, if we realize our reward in the future, then the pain we might experience in the present will not hinder our hope or jolt our joy (Romans 8:18-39, Hebrews 12:1-4). But what does it take to preserve this perspective? Nothing but to realize that it is not our *performance* but our *reliance* that makes us victors rather than victims, as Paul, while in prison himself, said "I can do everything through *him* who gives me strength (Philippians 4:13)," in addition to having said "For to me, to live is Christ, and to die is gain (Philippians 1:21)." This was as true for Paul in prison, as it was for the believers in Smyrna and it is for us today: If we suffer for Him, as He suffered for us, we will reign with Him as He rules forever (Rev. 22:5).

Are you faithful even to the point of death? If not, why not? What will you do to be done with your fear in order to move forward in true faith?

PUT LOVE FIRST

"Yet I hold this against you: You have forsaken your first love."

Revelation 2:4

Solid doctrine and good service, having the right answers and doing the right things, is nothing without the main thing: Christ Jesus wants not only our heads and our hands but our hearts. As soon as we base our security as a church, or as a believer, in knowing and doing the "right" things, we may not be "right" with God. Throughout the New Testament, we read about the need to develop a deep love for the Lord (see Matthew 22:37; Mark 12:30; Luke 10:27; John 14:15, 21:15-16; James 2:5; 1 Peter 1:8). If our love for God is not greater than our love for our closest relatives, including our children, our parents, our "best" friends, and even our spouses (1 Cor. 7:32-35), we may be guilty of the same sin as the Nicolaitions (Revelation 2:1-7), regardless of whether we engage in the acts of the Nicolaitions or any one who is living in a way that is morally compromising their convictions. We may be guilty of idolatry. Jesus calls us to change the attractions that are causing distractions between Him and us, both outwardly and inwardly. We are called to serve others not simply because it's the *right thing* to do, but because we love the *right One* for whom we do it. If not, then our "lampstand," or "light," will go out, and we will no longer be witnesses in this dark world. Our light would be extinguished, and we wouldn't clearly see the tree of life, but instead would taste death (2:7).

SYNCRETISM OR SACRIFICE

"I know where you live-where Satan has his throne. Yet you remain true to my name."

Revelation 2:13a

How good are you at standing firm without fear in the face of falsehood? The church in Pergamum did this well. It is often a challenge to love others enough to tell them what they *need* to hear regardless of what they *want* to ear. Yet, they did so, even at a moment of martyrdom (2:13b). However, they mixed good purposes with bad pleasures (2:14-16) and suffered as a result.

We often are tempted to continue to sin despite our salvation. When we see others compromising their convictions, we can easily fall into the same trap, if we are not vigilant (Galatians 6:1). To make matters worse, there are many people, including ourselves, who can "give ear" to things that are not of God or let our eyes and hearts set upon things that are of the devil. Astrology, false psychology, and pornography are only a few examples. We can call them what they truly are, sacrificing our "image" before others, or we can allow them to coexist with who we are, compromising our convictions before Christ. We can walk closely with Christ or stumble quickly with others.

The apostle Paul shared that "the time will come when people will not put up with sound doctrine. Instead, to suit their own desires, they will gather around them a great number of teachers to say what their itching ears want to hear. They will turn their ears away from the truth and turn aside to myths (2 Timothy 4:3, 4)." Sometimes the "teachers" we give ear to are in our own churches. Sometimes they are on our own televisions or radio stations or internet websites, chat rooms, or social media. Sometimes they are in our own homes. Sometimes they are in our own minds.

How can we keep ourselves from falling to the destruction of ourselves and the detriment of others? Remember where adherence to the teaching of Balaam led others-straight to their doom (Rev. 2:14; Numbers 25:1-9)! Remember that if we walk in the darkness, we will trip and fall. Yet, if we walk in the light of the Lord and His teachings, *obeying* His will for our daily lives rather than our own selfish will or the will of others, we will stand firm (1 John 1:5-1 John 2:6). If we don't walk what we talk and practice what we preach, not only when others are looking but when nobody is, we will surely reap what we sow.

Stand firm in Christ not only in your thoughts and words but also in your actions. If you do, then you too will "feed" your mind, body, and soul-not with food that tastes good in the mouth but then hurts the stomach (Job 20:12-15) but with food that only He can give, the "manna" that tastes good to your soul (Psalm 119:103; Rev. 2:17).

SPIRITUAL SCHIZOPHRENIA

"I know your deeds, your love and faith...Nevertheless, I have this against you: You tolerate that woman Jezebel, who calls herself a prophetess. By her teaching, she misleads my servants into sexual immorality..."

Revelation 2:19-20

In the name of "tolerance" for others, being tolerant not only of other people but also of their expressed thoughts that may or may not be in line with God's will, we can allow ourselves to be misled right into our own destruction. We can do good deeds, filled with love, true faith, a servant's heart, and a perseverant spirit (vs. 19), yet still be misled by our own appetites and the subtle deceptions imbedded in the teachings of others, whether intentional or not. As a result, we appear to be spiritually schizophrenic, with our words giving praise to Jesus but our hearts being far from Him. Case in point: If we admit that we are called to live holy lives, yet wink at sexual immorality from as blatant of a sin as adultery to as subtle of a sin as masturbation, we miss the point that we cannot walk in the Lord's ways when not only our bodies, but even our minds or our eyes are engaged in anything that would not be pleasing to Him. The Lord, whose "eyes are like blazing fire (vs. 18)," sees it all, reads our minds, and repays it (vs. 23a) unless it is paid for (vs. 23b).

The church in Thyatira learned this lesson the hard way. Those who allowed their minds to dwell on the things of the devil and then allowed their bodies to be engaged in the ways of this world were to be cast on a bed of suffering (vs. 22). The same is true for us today. Sin has its consequences, some seen and others unseen, some as obvious as sexual disease and others as hidden as emotional distress. Our only hope, as was theirs, is found in repenting from our sinful ways and others' selfish teachings, admitting our mistakes before Him and before others, so that we will be spared what we deserve (vs. 22) to receive that which we don't (Romans 6:23).

Repent of your old ways and renew yourself in His true ways, not only in your thoughts, but also in your words and actions! Then and only then will you take comfort in Jesus' words "To him who overcomes and does my will to the end, I will give authority over the nations-just as I have received authority from my Father (vs. 27)."

ASLEEP IN THE LIGHT

"I know your deeds; you have a reputation of being alive, but you are dead. Wake up!"

Revelation 3: 1c-2a

How can a church with a reputation for being alive be dead? Quite easily and unnoticeably. If we define being "alive" in terms of worldly measures, then we need only keep our seats filled during worship services and our lives busy during weekly endeavors to feel as if we are "alive." Yet, we could be as dead as a doorknob in the midst of it all. How? By doing what doesn't matter to the One for Whom we do it.

God is in the business of saving souls and reconciling his lost children to Himself. He can use us in the process if we are "worthy (vs. 4)" of being used by Him to bring transformation to the lives of others and glory to His. What makes us "worthy?" We are worthy when we have not "soiled (vs. 4)" our clothes, when we have not continued in our sin of growing only in knowledge of God's Word but not in obedience (vs. 3) to it. If our hearts are broken and our lives are open to His work in us and through us (Psalm 51:17), then nothing will stop Him from using us for His purposes (Romans 8:28, 29) in this world and in our lives. Then and only then will we truly be "alive."

The world is filled with churches that are full of activity and

15

housed in beautiful buildings but are often lacking evidence of eternal life. Why let your church become one of those churches? Keep the main thing the main thing: to grow in knowing Him and making Him known by the way you live your life. This is your spiritual act of worship (Romans 12:1, 2). This is how you will know that you are walking in His ways rather than your own, seeking His will rather than doing things in vain, walking with Him (vs. 4) rather than apart from Him or ahead of Him, walking in the light (1 John 1:10), rather than sleeping in it.

How are you walking, where are you walking, and why are you walking there? If you are walking with Christ, you will stay alive, carrying out His will for your life. If not, then apart from Him, you can do nothing that will raise yourself from your death (John 15:5). Walk with the Lord and be a blessing for Him, both now and always!

TRUE STRENGTH

"I know your deeds. See, I have placed before
you an open door that no one can shut. I know
that you have little strength, yet you have kept
my word and have not denied my name."

Revelation 3:8

What does it take to keep God's Word and to not deny His name? True strength, which is more internal than external, not stemming from a source within ourselves, but coming from a power above ourselves.

The church in Philadelphia was anything but strong in the worldly sense. For this and other reasons, it was often looked down upon by those who considered members of the church dismembers of the synagogue that purported to be true Jews, but were not (Romans 2:28-29; Rev. 2:9). As Jesus had said earlier to His disciples, a time would come when His followers would be kicked out of the synagogues on account of His name. The Apostle Paul had experienced such opposition, as many after him did too, and many still do today. Yet, when we rely on Christ rather than ourselves, He places before us an open door that "no one can shut (vs. 8)." When they think they can shut us out from God, He lets us in to His presence. No matter how much "stronger" they are than us, they are never strong enough to shut a door that only God can keep open. As Jesus said, "My sheep listen to my voice; I know them, and they follow me. I give them eternal life, and they shall never perish; no one can snatch them out of my hand (John 10:27, 28)."

The sad thing for those who try to shut the door is that they will one day realize that they are weak where they thought they were strong, bowing down to those who they thought were weak but are truly strong (vs. 9). Yet, they will do so when it's too late. If we too keep God's Word, growing not only in *knowledge* of it, but *obedience* to it (John 14:23), He will keep us not only *from*, but *through*, whatever trials we will face on this earth. We can rest assured in His ultimate protection of us, not knowing what the future holds, but knowing Who holds it, and acknowledging Him in the process, even when it is more costly than convenient.

Jesus said, "Whoever acknowledges me before men, I will also acknowledge him before my Father in heaven. But whoever denies me before men, I will deny him before my Father in heaven (Matthew 10:32, 33)." Who are you denying-yourself or our God? If we deny ourselves for the sake of our Savior, we will hold on to something that can never be taken away from us (vs. 11) as we carry on by His strength when we have none of our own (Philippians 4:13). If we deny our Savior for the sake of ourselves, we will lose it all and truly be weak. Which will you do?

FROM RAGS TO RICHES

"You say 'I am rich; I have acquired wealth and do not need a thing.' But you do not realize that you are wretched, pitiful, poor, blind and naked."

Revelation 3:17

We rejoice in God's provision and His promise that if we seek Him, His kingdom and His righteousness, everything else (we need) will be given to us as well (Matthew 6:33)! We may at times feel "rich" in many things: friends, property, prominence in the community, prosperity as a church. Yet, if we lose sight of the true riches of knowing Him and making Him known, we can easily fall into the trap in which the church in Laodicea found itself, going from riches to rags and not even realizing it (vs. 17).

What happened to them? They became lukewarm (vs. 16). They perhaps became so comfortable with their favor in the eyes of others that they lost favor in the eyes of God, as it is written, "Anyone who chooses to be a friend of the world becomes an enemy of God." (James 4:4b). We are called to be *in* this world but not *of* it. It's true that we want to make Christ known by demonstrating and offering Christ-like love, forgiveness and guidance to those who are longing to belong to Him but do not yet realize it. Yet, in doing so, we need to be careful not to befriend the ways of the world while befriending its people. We need to be the types of friends who lay down our

19

lives (John 15:13) for the sake of spearing others their deaths as they come to know the Author of Life not because of our compliance but because of our convictions.

If we are willing to walk not only in God's grace but also in His truth, then we will become "hot" rather than lukewarm to the point of boiling out the infirmities of our lives and the lives of others by the fire of God's Spirit working in us and through us. Are we willing to do so? Are you willing to do your part? If so, possessions and even property will continue to be simply a means to an end rather than the end itself and we will truly become "rich" in the process, relying more on our treasures in Heaven (Matthew 6:19-24) than those on earth.

BE SWIFT OR DRIFT

So often, when we have experienced a spiritual "high" in our walk with the Lord, we become susceptible to not being swift, or "ready," in guarding ourselves against the things that can bring us to a spiritual "low." When we allow ourselves to become prideful, rather than humble, we often learn the hard way that "...the pride comes before the fall (Prov. 11:2, 16:18)."

Case in point: Jacob. He had finally "gotten it right" with God (Gen. 32:22-32). Yet, while on his spiritual peak, he did not prepare himself for the valley that lay ahead. Soon, his daughter would be raped (Gen. 34:1-23), his sons would commit large-scale murder (Gen.24-31), and his authority would be jeopardized (Gen. 35:22). All of this happened after Jacob lied to his brother regarding following him to Seir (Gen. 33:14), stopping short of that destination by settling in Schechem (Gen. 33:18ff).

Jacob drifted away from God, placing his own will above the will of God, going through the motions of *religion* (Gen. 33:20) while losing sight of his *relationship* with the Lord. In fact, he lost so much sight of his significance in the eyes of the Lord that he became overly concerned about his image in the eyes of men (Gen. 34:30). As a result, he expressed more concern about his own well-being than the well-being of his daughter, a victim of rape.

Spiritual drift is dangerous because we often can fall under the lie that "I would never compromise God's plan for me (i.e. regarding singleness, marriage, work, parenting, etc.)," or "I will never, ever make a mistake like the one he/she/they made." The Apostle Peter, too, made this mistake when he exclaimed that he would "never" allow Jesus to be killed, saying, "This shall never happen to you (Matt. 16:22)." And yet if Jesus didn't go to the cross, fulfilling his long-awaited mission (Isaiah 53) Satan would have won the battle for our souls, as Jesus responded, "Get behind me Satan (Matt. 1623)!"

When Christ is at the periphery rather than the center of our lives, we can sometimes believe that God is leading us to do things He would never lead us to do (i.e. exercise bitterness, unforgiveness, deceit, abuse, an affair, divorce, greed, etc.). If we believe we are being spiritually led to think, say, or do something that contradicts God's Word, then we may be led by some spirit other than the Holy Spirit (1 John 4:1, Romans 12:2).

By whom are you led? How do you know for sure? What might you confess in turning over a new leaf on the tree of God's plan to empower you to become all that you were created to be (Romans 8:29, 1 John 1:9)? What better time than now to allow Christ to be not only a savior for your sins, but a leader for your life?

DEFEATING DEBT

*"Let no debt remain outstanding, except the
continuing debt to love one another..."*

Romans 13:8a

Each January, as we begin a new year, we may be feeling the affects of something that has been called one of the strongest religions of the postmodern era, the religion of consumerism. Consumerism is prevalent in our society today. Some of us may especially be feeling the affects of it as we receive our credit card charges for the previous month's purchases. Yet, even those of us who are not feeling particularly financially indebted are suffering consequences of consumerism nonetheless. One obvious evidence of the situation is what has become known as the "Health of Madison Avenue," or closer to home, it may be called the "Health of E-Bay." It is the sequence of wanting, getting, having, using, and trashing. We go from *wanting* something based on a perceived need, to *getting* it-at whatever costs to our family or our personal well-being. Once we have it we *use* it, and then we *trash* it, wanting something better-and the cycle continues. We have difficulty distinguishing between wants and needs, as advertisers tell us that our wants are our needs. We want, get, have, use, and trash everything from clothes, to furniture, to vehicles, to houses. And if we're not particularly materialistic, unfortunately, consumerism affects other areas of our lives too.

You see, consumerism has impacted our character. Many of us have an attitude of impatience. "I want what I want and I want it now!" We have a need for instant gratification. Even in the workplace, many of us want to start off at the top instead of first paying our dues. As a result, we have a reduced ability to enjoy, no satisfaction in "earning" something. The whole process of setting goals and taking steps to reach those goals is looked upon as a great big hassle, instead of a delightful challenge.

Consumerism has also impacted our values. Things are valued according to "usefulness." "What's it good for?" Our whole world is divided into useful/useless. Even people are valued according to usefulness. "How can this person help me get what I want?"-whether it's a promotion, a pay-raise, a house, children, sex, companionship, influence, the list can go on and on. Instead of loving people and using things, we often love things and use people. Even in the church. This leads to the writing off of certain people who we feel we just don't need to get ahead, or to get the amount of power we need at our workplace, or the amount of power we want in the church. The bottom line: Consumerism leads to the wanting, getting, having, using, and trashing of people. Our relationships with friends, wives, husbands, and children are affected. Marriage lasts as long as we're getting what we want; as soon as it gets costly, "I'm out of here. I'm gone. Who needs it, and who needs you?"

Consumerism has even impacted our relationship with God. We'd rather be served by Him than serve Him. "What can I get out of having a relationship with God?" Yet, God is not just another item on a list of consumer goods; God doesn't exist to serve us, we exist to serve God.

Perhaps our best new year's resolution this year would include assessing what we really need and questioning why we want what we want. As Jesus said, our lives do not consist in the abundance of our possessions (Luke 12:15). It's not what we own, but what owns us, that makes us who we are. This is why Paul calls greed "idolatry" (Colossians 3:5), as idolatry is worshiping something other than God *more* than God. If we are piled up in debt, chances are we might be looking for contentment in something other than Christ, in whom all true contentment exists. If the only debt we owe is the debt to love one another (Romans 13:8), then we are free to go where God wants us to go, to do what He calls us to do, owing nothing for anything or to anyone but the Lord.

HOW YOU HANDLE
WHAT YOU HANDLE

A Devotional based on Acts 5:1-11

"Now a man named Ananias, together with his wife Sapphira, also sold a piece of property. With his wife's full knowledge, he kept back part of the money for himself, but brought the rest and put it at the apostle's feet."

Acts 5:1-2

In light of the first recorded sin in the life of the New Testament church, we must be careful with how we handle what the Lord provides for us to handle.

To all appearances, Barnabas (see Acts 4:36-37) and Ananias did the same thing. Both sold property. Both brought the proceeds of the sale to the apostles, and both committed it to their disposal. The difference was that Barnabas brought *all* the sale money, while Ananias brought only a portion. Thus, Ananias and Sapphira perpetuated a double sin, a combination of dishonesty and deceit, as they led others to believe that they were giving all of what they received.

At first sight, there was nothing wrong in their withholding part of the sale money. As Peter plainly said later, their property was their own both before and after the sale (vs. 4). So they were under no obligation to sell their piece of land or, having sold it, to give away any-let alone all-of the proceeds. That is not the whole story, however. There's something else, something half-hidden. For Luke, in declaring that Ananias "kept back" part of the money for himself, chooses the verb nosphizomai, which means to "misappropriate." The same word was used in the earliest Greek translation of the Hebrew Old Testament (LXX) of Achan's theft, and in its only other New Testament occurrence it means to steal (Titus 2:10). We have to assume, therefore, that before the sale Ananias and Sapphira had entered into some kind of contract to give the church the total amount raised. Because of this, when they brought only some instead of all, they were guilty of embezzlement.

It was not on this sin that Peter concentrated, however, but on the other, hypocrisy. The apostle's complaint was not that they lacked honesty (bringing only a part of the sale price) but that they lacked integrity (bringing only a part, while pretending to bring the whole).

They were not so much misers as thieves and-above all-liars. They wanted the credit and the prestige for sacrificial generosity, without the inconvenience of it. So, in order to gain a reputation to which they had no right, they told a brazen lie.

Their motive in giving was not to relieve the poor, but to fatten their own ego. This is anything but walking humbly before God when it comes to financial dealings. They forgot that what others couldn't see, God could. They had anything but a strong sense of God's presence and His awareness of their motives. Rather than confessing their wrong motives, repenting and receiving His forgiveness, they thought they could pull a fast one on God. They were so worried about the ones who could see them in public and not in private that they showed no humility, and only foolish pride, in thinking they could escape the One who COULD see them in private.

No reply from Ananias to Peter's indictment and questions is recorded. Luke tells us only that God's judgment fell upon him: "he dropped dead." Understandably, fear seized the whole church. About three hours later, the incident repeated itself. Ignorant of her husband's death, Sapphira came in. Peter gave her a chance to repent by asking her to state the price they had received for the land, but she merely identified herself with his duplicity (vv. 7-8). So what happened to Sapphira? Peter warned her that those who had buried her husband would bury her too, and then she fell down at his feet and died.

What was the cause of all of this sin? Perhaps deep down inside, Ananias and Sapphira trusted more in their money, for all of their needs, than they did in God, who promised to meet those needs (Matthew 6:25-34). In light of where it led them, was it worth it? Perhaps the love of money, or the trust of money above and beyond trust in God, was the root of their evil. How about yours? Does your love and trust of Christ exceed your love and trust of money? If so, how is that demonstrated in your life? If not, what can you do to begin rising above what could hold you below in regard to your security in this life?

WHAT PLEASES GOD MOST

A Devotional based on Psalm 51

When we do wrong, we can wallow in our sin forever. David knew that well. He slept with Bathsheba, the wife of a member of his royal guard. It is ironic, or is it, that Bathsheba's husband's name was Uriah, meaning "My *light* is the Lord." David, meanwhile, tried to cover up his *darkness* by putting that light to death (see 2 Samuel 11:1-12:25, and in particular 11:14). Adultery and murder. Two "big" sins. And yet God's Word tells us that *anything* that separates us from Him is sin.

Scripture tells us that what David did deeply displeased the Lord. David hypocritically told Joab, Uriah's superior in the army, not to be "upset" about what happened to Uriah, as "war is war" and Joab could still go forward in battle without Uriah. But what David did (in his thoughts, words, and actions) displeased, or *upset* the LORD. In fact, in the Hebrew, there is a play on the words translated as "upset" in 2 Samuel 11:25 and "displeased" in 2 Samuel 11:27. The words sound very much alike. Why does this matter? It matters because, when reading this passage in its original language, a certain sound will come back to us. God poetically, through that sound, will help us dwell on the two words that make that sound. Those two words will then hopefully focus our attention on the main point, being that what we hope won't *upset* others usually *upsets* God.

This is why David, after becoming truly sorry for what he did, could say "Against you, you only, have I sinned and done what is evil in your sight... (vs. 4)." He realized that what he did not only harmed others and himself, but also harmed the heart of his loving Creator. He realized that his short-term pleasure caused a long-term pain in the heart of God. And he wondered what he could do to heal that hurt which now built a barrier between him and the Lord, causing his intimacy with God to diminish.

David learned, through his pain, that sin does have consequences for the individual who sins (2 Kings 14:6, John 3:36, Romans 6:23, etc.). So what could David do? And what could we do to right wrongs when we've sinned? Psalm 51 has the answer. The answer does not come from sacrifices of burnt offerings (vs. 16). It comes from the sacrifice of a burnt, or broken, heart (vs. 17).

David's sin was always on his mind (vs. 3), or "heart." He knew that God desires truth in the "inner parts (vs.6)" or "heart," and that God teaches us how to have wisdom in the "inmost place" (vs. 6), or "heart." This is why David sees that his only hope was not to offer something *external* (i.e. burnt offerings, money, time, merit-based works, etc.) but *internal* (a broken and contrite heart-vs.17). As a result, David cries out to the Lord for *God* to create in him a pure heart (vs.10), knowing he couldn't do it on his own. And we must do the same.

Is your heart broken before God? Is your spirit filled with joy because of His forgiveness? Is your service motivated by love and thanksgiving, rather than guilt and obligation? If not, why not? Won't you cry out to the Lord today, as "The Lord is near to the broken-hearted, and heals those who are crushed in spirit (Psalm 34:18)," and "If we confess our sins, He is faithful and just to forgive our sins and *purify* us of all unrighteousness (1 John 1:9)." Only then will transgressors be taught God's ways by us (vs. 13). Only then will sinners turn back to God (vs. 13), as they see the unknown Christ made known through our acceptance of God's forgiveness, His renewal of our spirit, and our willingness to let a broken and contrite heart lead us to a restored and renewed mind filled with His love for us, empowering us to love others.

AMAZING TOMORROWS

A Devotional based on Joshua Chapter 1

As the opening thoughts of this book expressed, while hiking, lost in the woods without a cell-phone, I could only call on God. I prayed and prayed. When my daughter Amanda who I was carrying exclaimed, "Daddy, I'm tired, hungry, and thirsty," I felt even worse than I already did regarding how "neglectful" I unintentionally had been. Yet, in the midst of my anxiety and fear, hidden not from God but from Amanda, the Lord brought me His peace, as He allowed Amanda to fall asleep in my arms. Perhaps she trusted that if Daddy was carrying her, she had nothing to fear, as she was still under my care. This was amazing to me. I prayed that not only today, but in all my tomorrows (if I had a "tomorrow"), my Father in heaven would amaze me with His care, as I rest in His arms.

What can make our "tomorrows" amazing? Remembering that God, our heavenly Father, is holding us in His arms no matter where we are or what we face. As He promised to Joshua, He promises to us, that He will never leave us or forsake us, as He will be *with* us (vs. 5). It was not until He assured Joshua of His presence, that He then exhorted Joshua to live his life on His promises. He commanded Joshua to obey His Word in order to enable His people to rise in unison to any challenges they would face together.

Likewise, His promise to you, as one who has faith in Him, is that He will be *"with* you (vs. 5)." The God of the universe, who has every right to remain *above* you in judgment, has chosen to be *with* you in Jesus, *if you choose to be with Him* (Joshua 24:15; John 14:23; Romans 9:33, 10:11-13). As the Apostle Paul asked, "If God is with us, who can stand against us (Romans 8:31)?" What other promise could we possibly want in our lives?

Amanda and I didn't know the way out of the wilderness. But we knew Who was with us in it. Once I trusted in His presence, He provided a way out (and a ride 11 miles back to where my car was parked!). He made possible what began to seem impossible, because He was with us. He does the same when we as a church, as individuals, as people who have surrendered to His will for our lives, trust in Him rather than ourselves.

What impossible possibility are you facing today? God offers to be with you in this endeavor. Are you with Him? What impossible possibility is God asking you to surrender to Him as a member of His body of believers? God wants to be with you in doing so. The question remains: Are you with Him? When we are disobeying God, we can become fearful, rather than courageous, as Joshua was told (1:6-9).

Is your life being lived in accordance with God's Word, His will for your life? If not, why not? Call upon the Lord to be with you, and He will answer. He will never leave you or forsake you. Pray to Him daily not only for His church but also for its members, and He will help you follow His will. Trust in Him in everything, and He will direct your path (Proverbs 3:5, 6), even out of any wilderness in which you may be today, so that you too can experience something amazing tomorrow.

DO WHATEVER YOU WANT WITH ME

A Devotional based on Luke 1:26-38

"Mary responded, 'I am the Lord's servant, and I am willing to accept whatever he wants. May everything you have said come true.' And then the angel left."

Luke 1:38

How many of us have the attitude of Mary? Being impregnated by the Holy Spirit, without others necessarily knowing the source of the pregnancy, can ruin any single and/or young woman's reputation for morally upright living. But it didn't ruin Mary's, at least not in the long run. Why? Because she knew that in the long run God would use her for His glory, to uphold His reputation, even at the expense of her own. She trusted that God would "have the last word" in showing the world that she didn't do anything wrong, but did everything right, in saying, as her baby would later say in His life on earth, "Not my will but Yours be done (Matthew 26:39)."

Doing things God's way, surrendering to His will for our lives, rather than our own, even at great personal cost, is the only way by which we will become all that we were created to be (Psalm 40:8;143:10, Isaiah 53:10, Matthew 6:10; 7:21; 12:50;26:42, John 6:38;7:17, Romans 12:1-2, Philippians 2:13,

Hebrews 10:7, 1 John 5:14, Revelation 4:11). Without doing so, it is impossible to do what God wants us to do in our lives. This may be difficult and overwhelming at times, but if we embrace any pain rather than erase it, contrary to what society may tell us, we may learn in a more personal way that "With God all things are possible (1:37),"as the angel told Mary. Mary was willing to do so, and as a result rejoiced in the opportunity to face hardship, not only physically but also emotionally and spiritually, for the sake of knowing God and making Him known.

How about you? To what extent are you willing to go in order to find the true fulfillment and contentment in your life that you can only have through surrendering not only your body, but also your heart and your mind for God's ways rather than your ways or the ways of this world? The extent to which you do so is directly proportionate to the extent to which you will live the life of "abundance (John 10:10)" for which Christ Jesus came into the world in the first place. It's all up to you-yet you are not alone in your decision (Philippians 2:13). What will you do?

WHEN DOUBT DAMPERS DOING

"I do believe; help me overcome my unbelief!"

Mark 9:24b

When we read the account of the father of a demon-possessed boy expressing his doubts to Jesus regarding Jesus' ability to heal his son, we can almost hear the tone of disappointment in Jesus' voice. The boy's father said "...if you can do anything, take pity on us and help us (Mark 9:22b)." Jesus responded, "*If* you can? Everything is possible for him who believes." It is almost as if Jesus was disgusted and frustrated with the man's lack of faith. Jesus made it clear that the true question was not whether He had the power to heal the boy, but whether the boy's father had faith to believe it.

A person who truly believes will set no limits on what God can do. When Jesus said "The faith of a mustard seed can move mountains (Matthew 17:20, 21)," He was not concerned with the *amount* of faith one has, but rather with the *type* of faith one has. Is it the type of faith that relies on human power, or the type that requires trust in divine intervention? If our faith is in Christ, rather than in ourselves, we have no need to doubt, as God can do anything (Matthew 19:26). We can have the type of faith that never questions God's power. Yet, when we rely on our own power, we soon find out that we are powerless in regard to bringing about changes that heal the hurt of our lives or the lives of those we love.

36

When the disciples asked Jesus why they were not able to drive out the demon, Jesus said, "This kind can come out only by prayer (vs. 29)." Does that mean that other types of demons can come out without prayer? Maybe. But maybe not. Although "this kind" seems to imply that there are different types of demons in people's lives, "only by prayer" reminds us that we can so easily forget the source of our power. We can take for granted the power given to us through Christ by the Holy Spirit. We can easily forget to first "pray," to first "consult with God," in order to ask for power over demonic spirits, or anything else that holds people in bondage. This includes the power to move forward in our lives by faith rather than fear, as the father of the boy realized when he finally asked *Jesus* to help him overcome his unbelief (vs. 24b). He realized that the only true "help" comes from the Healer Himself, and must be requested in humility and in hope.

The disciples may have missed the boat. Rather than praying before acting, they acted before praying, and were humbled as a result (vs. 28). They learned the hard way that it is better to first speak to God about others before speaking to others about God. Only then can we be sure that the type of faith we have is the type of faith that comes from seeking first God's will, building His kingdom rather than our own (Matthew 6:33). This type of faith is based not on our ability, but our availability to the One through whom we can do all things (Philippians 4:13).

THE GIFTS AND THE GIVER

A Devotional based on I Corinthians 12:1-3

In our use of the gifts, we can easily lose sight of the Gift-Giver. That's what happened in the Corinthian church. Their use of the gifts perhaps became a demonstration of their own power rather than God's. Today, in a cultural mentality of the "survival of the fittest," the church can easily become unfit to positively impact a culture that has negatively impacted us. We live in a culture in which selfish gain for personal happiness rather than selfless giving for personal holiness is often what determines how we live our lives, whether or not we realize it. It can also dictate our behavior not only in our workplaces and homes, but also in our ministries and church. If we allow this to continue, we will negate the power of the Gospel to set others free from the things (namely sin, selfishness, and Satan) that are keeping them from becoming all they were created to be. When people look at us, they will see nothing different than what they see elsewhere in this world.

How can we overcome this dilemma? We can refuse to confuse spiritual gifts with spirituality. We can remember that the fruit of the Spirit (Galatians 5:22-23) always takes precedence over the gifts of the Spirit, and that true spirituality has more to do with building up others in the Spirit of God's love (1 Corinthians 13) rather than building up ourselves in a spirit of our pride. By reflecting upon how we live each moment of each day, whether at the beginning or the end of that day, we can replace the lies of this world with the truth of God's Word through reading His Word, taking on His attitude towards others, and confessing where we have gone wrong in order to receive mercy from Him and others who can hold us accountable to a new way of living (Proverbs 28:13, 1 John 1:8, 9). We can also grow in our knowledge of the spiritual gifts in order to grow in obedience to God's leading in our lives when it comes to our unique role in the body of Christ. By doing so, we will be empowered to use whatever gift we have to serve others, rather than to be served by them (Matthew 20:28), in a special way, in *our own* special way, as members of the body of Christ (1 Peter 4:10). If we are ignorant about the use or misuse of spiritual gifts, we can use them to draw others closer to ourselves rather than Christ. But if we refuse to be ignorant, we will have our eyes fixed on Christ, the Gift-Giver, rather than ourselves, the recipients of the gifts.

Pray that God will display His extraordinary powers through our ordinary lives so that others will be drawn *to* Him rather than *away from* Him when they see how we use what He has given us for their well-being and His glory rather than ours.

UNITY VERSUS UNIFORMITY

A Devotional based on I Corinthians 12:4-11

What's the difference between unity and uniformity? True unity doesn't require uniformity in meeting a common goal. God's goals may be mysterious when it comes to understanding His purpose for our particular paths in life. Yet, His goal is clear when it comes to determining His purpose for the church: "Go therefore and make disciples of all nations..." (Matthew 28:19,20). We can only fulfill this great commission by being empowered by the Holy Spirit individually in order to serve as God's witnesses collectively, as Christ Jesus said "...you will receive power when the Holy Spirit comes on you; and you will be my witnesses in Jerusalem, and in all of Judea and Samaria, and to the ends of the earth" (Acts 1:8).

Much of the power of the Holy Spirit comes in the form of the gifts of the Holy Spirit. Yet, in our use of these gifts, the saying that "united we stand, divided we fall" holds true for the church perhaps even more so than for other organizations. Why? Because Jesus Himself said that non-believers will know that we belong to Him not by our gifts but by our fruit (Matthew 7:20); the fruit of love leading to unity being the greatest of them all (1 Corinthians 13:13). This makes us true witnesses of Christ.

This great witness of Christ in us and through us as a body of believers can only take place when we have unity in the midst of diversity. Unlike uniformity, unity doesn't require that we all look, act, and think the same way, nor does having one voice require that we all sound the same. Rather, unity requires that diversity doesn't become a threat but a treat. It requires that we learn to appreciate one another's differences rather than to be threatened or annoyed by them. It also requires that we accept the gifts God has given us, not wishing that we had someone else's gifts, nor thinking that we can choose *our* gifts, but realizing that the Gift-Giver saw fit to give us just what we have in order to fulfill the purpose He has.

You are needed by the church in order for the church to fulfill its purpose, and yet you need the church in order to fulfill yours. Although the church is not complete without you, you are not complete without the church. Yet, God is sovereign in determining your role in the grand scheme of things. And although we may not understand how God picks and chooses who does what in the body of believers, we can have unity in fulfilling our purpose when we're more concerned about the "common good" (vs. 7) than our own. That is His hope for you.

LOVE LASTS

A Devotional based on I Corinthians 13:1-13

The right way in which we are to use all spiritual gifts is the way of love. Why? Because the fruit of the Spirit (Galatians 5:22, 23) always takes precedence over the gifts of the Spirit (1 Corinthians 12) and love is the ultimate fruit. Even the most powerful use of the gifts of tongues, prophecy, faith, and giving are powerless if used without love (vv. 1-3).

God's type of love, *agape* love, is characterized by a selfless concern for the well being of others not based on how loving they are but how willing we are. If we are willing to love others as Christ loves us (John 13:34), then we see that love involves action not feeling, the ultimate action being that we lay down our lives for others as Christ laid down His life for us (1 John 3:16). Yet, it's often easier to die physically than it is to die to ourselves. But if we don't die to ourselves, we may be known more by our gifts than our fruit, following ourselves more than Christ, as Christ said that those who follow Him will be known not by their knowledge or gifts but their fruit (John 13:35).

Faith involves believing without seeing, and we are blessed because of it (John 20:29). Yet, it is based on what has not yet come. Hope is not unfounded wishful thinking, but involves waiting on the return of our Lord Jesus Christ (Titus 2:11-14). Yet, what we hope for will one day be fully received (Hebrews

6:13-18). We read, "And now these three remain: faith, hope and love. But the greatest of these is love (vs. 13)." Faith and hope will one day no longer be necessary, as faith will be realized and hope will be fulfilled. But love will always remain. Even after the gifts are no longer necessary, love will still be the guiding element that fuels all that God and His people are and do.

NON-CONFORMISTS

A Devotional based on Romans 12:1-8

We worship by the way we live our lives (vv. 1-2). This requires not only keeping our physical bodies from sin (Romans 6:13) but also keeping our spiritual body, as a body of believers, from corruption. This is only possible by using our gifts for God's purposes rather than our own. If we seek His will, and pray for His will (Matthew 6:9-10), even if it conflicts with our own, then it will be done. If not, we are not truly worshiping Him, but may be worshiping ourselves, or another, as we obey the desires of whomever or whatever we worship (Joshua 24:15; John 14:23; Romans 6:12).

If we conform to the ways of this world (vs. 2a), we will relate to one another the way the rest of the world does-with selfishness and pride, building our own little kingdom rather than God's. But if we instead are "transformed by the renewing of our mind (vs. 2b)," we will respond to one another in a way that demonstrates more concern for the well being of others than ourselves (1 Corinthians 12:7). Then and only then can we be sure that what we are doing, not only as believers but also as a church, is being done in accordance with God's will and is not being done in vain (vs. 2).

If we think our way is the only way, whether in regard to how a ministry is carried out or in regard to who would carry it out, we are probably thinking too highly of ourselves (vs. 3).

None of us holds the corner on the market when it comes to prophesying, serving, teaching, preaching, encouraging, giving, leading or showing mercy (vv. 6-8), or any other gift. If we say, whether outwardly or inwardly, that "Unless someone leads, or preaches, or serves the way I do, then...," we are deceiving ourselves, as each person is held accountable for using their gifts according to their own faith and understanding (vs. 6), not yours.

Let's not judge others or ourselves wrongly (Matthew 7:1-6), but leave ourselves and our lives in the hands of the only true Judge, and, "in view of His mercy (vs. 1)," show that mercy to one another. Then and only then will we truly empower every member to be a minister (Ephesians 4:11, 12) just as God wants us to do. Then and only then will we remember that we can only successfully unwrap and use our gifts if we recognize that gifts are not earned but given (vv. 3 & 6), not by our efforts but by God's grace, to be used not only in His will but also in His ways.

THE SPIRIT ABOVE THE SPIRITS

A Devotional based on Acts 2:1-4; Ephesians 5:18-21

The question is not "Do I have all of the Holy Spirit," but "Does the Holy Spirit have all of me?" If He does, then any "wind" (Acts 2:2) that results in the process would come from the Lord and not from us.

Sometimes we must not only honestly reflect upon our own source of power but also prayerfully discern the source of seemingly spiritual activity in and through others. Why? Because a person who seems to be full of the Spirit just might be full of a spirit, but not the Holy Spirit. After all, Jesus said that we will know who is led by His Spirit by the fruit they bear (Matthew 7:20). The "bad fruit" that one could bear, especially in the use of the "sign" gifts, is sometimes the fruit of bringing more attention to themselves than to Christ. These people appear to be "holy" and very "spiritual," but are in actuality putting themselves on the throne that only Christ belongs upon, or perhaps simply allowing others to exalt them above other human beings, when we are all on level ground at the foot of the cross (see Philippians 2:3).

Jesus said, "Many will say to me on that day 'Lord, Lord, did we not prophesy in your name, and in your name drive out demons and perform many miracles?' Then I will tell them plainly 'I never knew you. Away from me, you evildoers!'" (Matthew 7:22-23). How can this be? How can a person who seems so "spiritual," who seems to be working for the Lord, actually be working for themselves, or even for the devil? How can this be so if that person also drives out demons and performs miracles in Jesus' name? According to Scripture, demons can be driven out, and even miracles can be performed, apart from the power of the Holy Spirit, even by people who appear to know Christ Jesus well, yet are far from Him (Isaiah 29:13; Matthew 15:8-9). Jesus warns us to watch out for these deceivers who are often simply deceived themselves, not even knowing that they are deceiving others. The Apostle Paul tells us that these people are often simply filling their own appetites for power, prestige, position, or authority over others (see Philippians 3:18-19; 1 Timothy 4:1-2, and elsewhere). Their "power" is ultimately powerless.

So how can we tell when a person's power is from the Holy Spirit versus some other spirit? How can we discern if our own power is from God and not ourselves? We can see the fullness of the Spirit in us when our lives demonstrate humility and grace rather than pride and arrogance, whether outward or inward (Philippians 2:5-11). We can consider whether or not our lives consistently bring others into a worship of Christ and not ourselves. We can reflect upon whether we submit to others out of reverence for Christ (Ephesians 5:21) or if we respect others out of reverence for organizational, political, or worldly power, whether in the home, workplace, church, or elsewhere.

If we are not "filled" or "controlled" by the Holy Spirit, we will be using our gifts and all that God entrusts to us not out of an overflowing well, but one that will soon dry up, because its source is ultimately useless for demonstrating the power of

God in us and through us. Therefore, if we are full of the Spirit, we will glorify Christ, but if we are full of ourselves, He will nullify us (Proverbs 11:2). Be filled with the Spirit and enjoy His guidance that leads to true happiness in the long run!

FROM CONDEMNATION TO COMPASSION

A Devotional based on Luke 10:25-37

There was a man in New York who asked his pastor what he must do to inherit eternal life. His pastor, a very wise and discerning man, responded not with an answer, but with another question: "What does the Bible say? How do you read it?" The lawyer answered, "Accept Jesus Christ as my Lord and Savior, seeking His will for my life." The pastor responded, "You have answered correctly. Do so and you will be saved." But the lawyer wanted to justify himself, so he asked his pastor, "How can anyone know for sure that he or she is seeking and following the Lord's will in a given situation?"

In reply, the pastor said: "A man was driving along the Bronx Expressway one evening when his car broke down. The very feared 'Bronx strippers' came to strip his car apart in order to sell its parts for cash. They also beat up the motorist, stripped him of his expensive suit, taking his wallet and house keys, leaving him half dead."

"An evangelical protestant minister drove by, looking the other way, remembering that he had to be at his next meeting in ten minutes and was already running late. A woman who was 'born again' and an active member of a nearby community church also drove by, saw the man calling out for help, and kept on driving. But a member of an outspokenly gay and

49

lesbian church in Manhattan, as she traveled, came where the man was; and when she saw him, was filled with compassion towards him. She went to him, and bandaged his wounds with supplies from her first-aid kit. Without a cell-phone to call an ambulance, she dragged the man into her car, and brought him to the nearest hospital. Arriving at the hospital, she was asked for his insurance card, as they would not admit anyone without an insurance card or a very large cash outlay. Because his insurance card along with his wallet was stolen, she gave them her credit card with $10,000 of available credit, saying, 'Please take care of him. Charge me whatever the costs are. If there are more charges than $10,000, I will pay them in full tomorrow when I stop in on my way to work. Here are my work and home telephone numbers if you need to reach me.'

"The pastor asked, 'Which of these three do you think was following the Lord's will in this situation?' The lawyer answered, 'The one who had mercy on the wounded motorist.' The pastor told him, 'Go and do likewise.'"

When it comes to doing God's will, Jesus told us in all things to "…do to others what you would have them do to you, for this sums up the Law and the Prophets (Matthew 7:12)." Treating others as we would want them to treat us, known as the "Golden Rule," is God's will for all of us who want to live His plan for our lives. We so often get caught up in the details of life's decisions while losing sight of the big picture. The big picture of God's will for our lives is summed up in Romans 8:29 in which the Apostle Paul reminds us that God wants us to become more like Christ, in whom we will have true contentment and fulfillment in this life and the next. Yet, often, we ask the wrong questions.

The lawyer mentioned in Luke 10:25-29 asked, "Who is my neighbor?" Jesus showed him that the better question is, "Am *I* a neighbor to others?" In fulfilling the Golden Rule, we will become more like Christ, with the help of the Holy Spirit, who empowers those who are not just "hearers of the word," but "doers" of it (James 1:22). Let's not get caught up in the minute details of our lives, but rather, let's focus on the major decisions of our hearts. In so doing we will become more like Christ, God's ultimate will for all of us.

In Jesus' day, a Samaritan would be condemned by the devout, God-fearing priests and Levites, who sometimes considered Samaritans not only "half-breeds," with half the truth and half the lies, but also the "scum of the earth." The very fact that Jesus would paint a "Samaritan" in a good light would have shaken up any devout "religious" person of that day. Yet, the very people they would condemn, Jesus would commend, if they were people of compassion. Did He agree with their sinful life-styles? No. Did He condone their false doctrines? No. Would I agree with someone who claims to be an "evangelical practicing homosexual" on doctrinal issues dealing with sexual immorality? No. But Jesus challenged the lawyer to see in others' hearts, even the heart of a particular "Samaritan," what we need in ours: Compassion.

As we read elsewhere, "Jesus, when He saw the crowds, had compassion on them, because they were harassed and helpless, like sheep without a shepherd (Matthew 9:36)."

If we want to make the unknown Christ known, and follow the will of God in our decisions, then we must make every decision, regardless of its implications, with the type of compassion that will bring us to action, rather than inaction, in healing the wounded. Their wounds may be physical, emotional, or spiritual. Yet, only when we decide to bring healing, not harm, to their wounds, will we truly make the invisible Christ visible not only by our words but also by our actions. Only then will we be known not by our condemnation of others, but by our compassion for them (John 3:17, 13:34, 35).

GETTING UP WHEN YOU'RE DOWN

A Devotional based on 2 Corinthians 1:3-11

Second Corinthians is a personal letter from the Apostle Paul to the believers in Corinth. It's a lot like a letter you might write to a close friend. Paul was sharing his heart with a church he loved. In verses 3 through 7, the words "comfort" or "consolation" appear 10 times. What does this mean? The words "suffering," "afflicted," or "tribulation" appear 6 times. What is God telling us by the many times He uses the words comfort and suffering in this passage? I think He is telling us that, although we will suffer in this world, especially as Christ-followers, if we turn to Him, He will somehow give us more than enough comfort in our sufferings, so that we can use that extra comfort to help others who are in need of comfort. In such a way, we can turn a weakness into a strength, if we pray for and look for opportunities to do so.

When I've been depressed, I've sometimes found admitting it to be very difficult. What would people think if a seminary graduate serving as an ordained minister who sometimes counsels depressed people were to be depressed? For a while I felt shame. Yet, once I admitted that I was depressed, some relief came from the confession itself. I learned to "cry out" to God. I also realized that part of my healing was the "crying out" itself.

God truly wants to hear from us, especially during times of trouble. Yet, He also wants us to trust Him to deliver us from those troubles. Yet, this deliverance takes time, His time, healing time.

The apostle Paul was depressed. Many of us consider the apostle Paul to have been a spiritual superman. "Surely such a giant of the faith could not be overcome by depression!" Yet, when we look at his words, we see otherwise. Describing his and Timothy's condition while in Asia he says, "We were under great pressure, far beyond our ability to endure, so that we despaired even of life. Indeed, in our hearts we felt the sentence of death (vv. 8b-9a)." Looking at the Greek, I might translate Paul's words to read, "we were so utterly, unbearably depressed that we wanted to die." In other words, it was probably hard for Paul to get out of bed in the morning, if he had a bed, to face another day.

How would you like such thoughts to describe your life? Perhaps they do at this time, or will at some time in the future. But there is hope! Be comforted in the fact that people like Paul, who we might consider a "super-saint," but who considered himself the "chief of sinners (1 Tim. 1:15)," along with many other Christ-followers, experienced extreme discouragement and depression, and yet survived! How did he do it?

He told somebody (2 Cor. 1:8-9). He trusted in God (vs. 9). He remembered that God is a Deliverer (vs. 10). Finally, he asked for help, as he mentioned how important the Corinthians' prayers were to him (vs. 11).

When you are struggling with discouragement or depression, intimate relationships with God and others are essential.

54

It is crucial that we enlist fellow believers as intercessors and burden-sharers. In doing so, you might find that one or two of them may have experienced depression themselves. Just seeing them could help you make it through your day. Their presence, without any words, could give you hope. Their presence will touch you and minister to you. Ultimately, their presence can be a reminder of the truth that our Savior and Lord, Jesus Christ, also struggled with depression. In fact, the "man of sorrows (Isaiah 53)," who overcame all things, even depression, can empower us to do the same. That is my prayer for you.

GOD'S DESIGN FOR COMMUNITY

A Devotional based on Acts 2:42-47

Whether or not we admit it to others, if we're honest with ourselves, we may admit that we all need others in our lives. And deep down inside, we all want to belong. We all want to find our place in this world. And when we don't, we often suffer from a lack of self esteem, as we see ourselves as less and less desirable to be with, or we strive to convince ourselves and others, including potential marriage partners, friends, or in-laws, that we are desirable to be with. We often wear many masks to try to keep others from finding out what we are really like and how imperfect we really are. We can do this by hiding from others, physically or emotionally, in order for them to not see who we really are. Even those of us who have become Christ-followers often struggle with this dilemma. It seems, even though we may have a spouse, a job, children, a place to live and a car to drive, a great stereo system, a camcorder and internet access, that something else is still missing. What is that something else? That something else is true community. We all need true community, Christ-centered community, in our lives. And why do we need it? The Word of God offers us an answer to these questions.

First, it helps us develop a better sense of identity (Acts 2:42-43). We can base our identity on many things. Yet, until we base it on Christ, we have no true sense of who we were created to. The early Christians had their identity in its proper place. They devoted themselves to the apostles' teaching. This teaching, with timeless truths, is what we have recorded today in our New Testament. Through the Gospel message, they learned who they were in Christ. They learned that they were relational beings created in the image of a relational God, and as such, were invaluable in His eyes. They learned that through Christ's death on the cross they were forgiven for not being perfect, they were forgiven for all of their sins, and were offered a chance to start all over again (2 Corinthians 5:17), as they accepted Christ's payment on the cross for their sins (John 3:16). Also, they were empowered by the Holy Spirit to live the life they were created to live.

Second, the early Christians enjoyed corporate fellowship with other believers once a week and small group fellowship even more often than that (vs. 46). This helped them to see that they were not "in it alone." As we read in Romans 12:4-5, "Just as each of us has one body with many members, and these members do not all have the same function, so in Christ we who are many form one body, and each member belongs to all the others."

Third, they broke bread together to commemorate what Christ did for them on the cross. Without doing so, it would have been easy for them to forget that their significance is not based on power, prestige, position, or possessions, but rather, it was based upon the love and forgiveness of Jesus Christ. Rather than focusing on whether or not they were able to please others, they sought to please Him.

Fourth, they prayed-they communicated with God. They learned to not only experience the "abundant life" (John 10:10) that Christ offered to them while they were on this earth, but also to look forward to the eternal life that they would have after leaving this earth (John 5:24).

We can do the same. We too can know who we are through the same means. We too can become better able to answer the question of "Who am I?" When we are in Christ, we are a new creation. Rather than simply plugging God into the formula of our lives, we plug into His life to find our true identity with Him. As His children, and with the power of the Holy Spirit, we no longer have to conform to the ways of this world (Romans 12:2). As a result, we will be *in* this world but not *of* it, living for His glory rather than for ours (Matthew 5:14-16). Also, our relationships with one another will be unlike those outside of the body of believers. Our relationships will be characterized by intimacy, commitment, unity and love (vv. 44-47a).

The early Christians offered their lives to Christ. Their lives then had true meaning and purpose. They had the purpose, as we do today, to win other souls to Him, as He is always looking for others to join His community: "This is good, and pleases God our Savior, who wants everybody to be saved and come to a knowledge of the truth (1 Timothy 2:3-4)." And win them they did! Verse 47 of our passage tells us that the Lord added to their number daily! They were such an incredible witness of God's power and love that people were drawn to them in large numbers. They had a sense of purpose *and* direction.

We too have the same mission. Our calling is to share the great news of God's forgiveness and new life in Christ with those who do not yet know Him (Matthew 18:19, 20). How are we doing in carrying out such a great calling? How are you doing in using your particular gifts for this great purpose?

HE WHO DIES WITH THE MOST TOYS...

A Devotional based on Psalm 49

Unfortunately, many of us have seen those bumper stickers that tell us "He who dies with the most toys wins." Worse yet, some of us have even believed this statement. Yet, Psalm 49 has a different message for us. Psalm 49 reminds us that nobody ever saw a hearse pulling a U-Haul. As we read, "Do not be overawed when a man grows rich, when the splendor of his house increases; for he will take nothing with him when he dies, his splendor will not descend with him (vv. 16, 17)." We simply can't take with us into eternity what belongs to us here on earth. And our worldly status will not insure our heavenly significance.

Why is this hard to remember? Perhaps because we live in a society in which the "Health of Madison Avenue" often deceives us into gaining a false sense of security. The sequence of wanting, getting, having, using, and trashing can consume us as we consume things that will not last. We go from *wanting* something based on a perceived need, to *getting* it-at whatever costs to our family budget or our personal well-being. Once we *have* it we *use* it, and then we eventually *trash* it, wanting something better-and the cycle continues. We have difficulty distinguishing between wants and needs, as advertisers tell us that our wants are our needs. We want, get, have, use and trash everything from clothing to furniture, to cars and houses. As a result, we live in the days of two incomes, but more divorce; of fancier houses, but broken homes.

You see, consumerism has impacted our character. Many of us have an attitude of impatience. "I want what I want and I want it now!" We have a need for instant gratification. Even in the workplace, many of us want to start off at the top instead of first paying our dues at the bottom.

Consumerism has also impacted our values. Things are valued according to "usefulness." "What's it good for?" Our whole world is divided into useful/useless. Even people are valued according to usefulness. "How can this person help me get what I want?," Whether it's a promotion, a pay-raise, a house, children, sex, companionship, the list can go on and on. Instead of loving people and using things, we often love things and use people. Even in the church. This leads to the writing off of certain people who we feel we just don't need to get ahead, or to get the amount of power we need at our workplace, or the amount of power we want in the church. Consumerism leads to the wanting, getting, having, using, and trashing of people. Our relationships with friends are affected. Marriage lasts as long as we're getting what we want; as soon as it gets costly, "I'm out of here. I'm gone. Who needs it, and who needs you?"

Consumerism has even impacted our relationship with God. We'd rather be served by Him than to serve Him. As long as He allows us to have what we want, we are willing to forsake what we need, relying on ourselves instead of Him. All of this stems from trusting in things that are created rather than the One who ultimately created them, trusting in ourselves rather than our God: "But man, despite his riches, does not endure; he is like the beasts that perish. This is the fate of those who *trust in themselves*... (vv. 12-13a)."

Is it bad to "have?" Is it a sin to be rich? I don't think that it is, as God's Word tells us that it is the *love* of money that is the source of much evil (1 Timothy 6:10), not having the money itself. It is what we do with what we have that shows us *whose* we are. Those who do not rely on their worldy riches but their heavenly treasures belong to God. Those who don't, belong to death, both temporarily and eternally (vs. 14).

Jesus said, "Do not store up for yourselves treasures on earth, where moth and rust destroy, and where thieves break in and steal. But store up for yourselves treasures in heaven, where moth and rust do not destroy, and where thieves do not break in and steal. For where your treasure is, there your heart will be also (Matthew 6:19-21)." Where is your heart?

We can sometimes believe that something we possess will bring us peace and something we buy will keep us safe. We trust in everything from the latest technology in our offices to the greatest security systems in our homes. Yet, unforeseen catastrophes are a reminder that even the greatest of worldly wealth can't buy us the safest of spiritual security. Only Jesus Christ can do that (John 5:24). And He did, for all those who trust not in themselves (vs. 13), but in Him (vs. 15; John 14:1ff.), not only for their salvation (John 3:16) but also for their signifi-cance (Matthew 6:25-34). In what will you trust? I hope and pray you will trust in Him.

He who dies with the most toys still dies. But where will he go when he dies?

HOW CAN I SHARE MY FAITH WITHOUT EMBARASSING GOD?

A Devotional based on 1 Peter 3:15, 16

Sometimes it seems as if "do as I say, not as I do!" has become a dangerous cliché in our culture. Hypocrisy has been a major obstacle to the faith of a seeker who is looking for hope in Christ while being stumbled by Christians. Feeling as if we cannot "walk what we talk" or "practice what we preach" often keeps us from sharing what we believe with others who are looking for something to believe. Worse yet, our lack of consistency in living our lives according to *what we believe* rather than *how we feel* can mislead those who are looking to us for hope in a hopeless world.

I once heard a preacher tell other preachers that if you can't "dazzle them with brilliance, then baffle them with baloney." Actually, he used another word. But the point was that this particular preacher was not practicing what he preached. Instead of exercising integrity he was utilizing deceit. This stumbled me, as a young man who was preparing for vocational ministry. I was forced to ask "How can I prevent myself from being a hypocrite?," knowing that I will fail to always be consistent in my witness of Christ, as my position in Christ may be perfect (Romans 8:1-4), but my condition is far from it (Romans 7:18, 8:29). Peter gives us an answer to this agonizing question.

In 1 Peter 3:16a, Peter reminds us that we become free from fear, or anything else that keeps us from sharing our faith with others, by "keeping a clear conscience." A clear conscience allows us to share without fear, knowing that we may not be perfect, but are being perfected daily (Hebrews 12:1-2), as even Jesus was "made perfect" through His trials (Hebrews 5:8, 9). When Jesus resisted the temptation to not walk what He talked, the temptations He faced were real and the battle for victory was difficult. Yet, where Adam failed, Jesus prevailed. Jesus' humanity was completed, "made perfect," in order to be able to give us the power to do the same. It is not that in Christ it is impossible to sin, but in any given circumstance, it is possible not to sin. By living with a higher level of consistency in walking what we talk, not only in our actions but in our attitudes (Matthew 7:1-5), we will gain a clearer conscience, enabling us to more boldly share what others need to hear. You and I will be less of a discouragement and more of an encouragement to the faith of others, especially those who "...ask you to give the reason for the hope that you have (1 Peter 3:15b)."

Are you sharing faith in Christ regularly with those who are seeking it? If not, why not? What barriers are in your way, whether internal or external? If so, how are you sharing your faith? Are you doing so with conviction or condemnation? Are you sharing with harshness and disrespect, or gentleness and respect (vs. 15)? Are you filled with faith or filled with fear? Remember the truth of 1 John 4:18, "There is no fear in love. But perfect love drives out fear, because fear has to do with punishment. The one who fears in not made perfect in love."

God's love is such that He wants to share His message, through you His messenger, with lost people (John 3:16, 17), as lost people matter to God (2 Peter 3:9). If you are sharing His message, not only visually by the way you live your life, but verbally by the way you communicate His good news, then you are walking in His love. If not, you may be falling in your fear. Let's not forget that lost people need to not only *see* the Good News, but *hear* it too (Romans 10:14-17).

WHERE IS GOD WHEN IT HURTS?

A Devotional based on Psalm 22

Did you know that the anguished prayer of a godly sufferer feeling *torn inside* and *tossed aside* by God, Psalm 22, found in the Old Testament, is quoted in the New Testament more than any other Psalm? When we learn this, we can't help but wonder why.

Perhaps it is because no other psalm was as fitting to the circumstances of Jesus Christ at His crucifixion than was Psalm 22. In Jesus, we see the ultimate fulfillment of the cry of a faithful person in a faithless world and the agony of a person who cries out for mercy but finds nothing but judgment. It is the cry of one who seemingly suffers endlessly, needlessly, and sometimes shamefully. It is the cry of one who loses family, fame, fortune, and sometimes even faith while weathering life's storms. It is the cry of one whose situation simply does not seem to be fair, especially while believing in a God who is just. It is the cry of having no hope in the midst of hopelessness. It is the cry we cry when we can't answer the question "why?" It is the cry that sometimes makes us want to die because we feel as if God has abandoned us, forsaken us, and maybe even forgotten us.

When the Old Testament patriarch, Job, lost his good reputation, great riches, and closest relatives, he commented on the hard times of humanity in general, and his own situation in particular (Job 7). He was distressed and distraught, displeased and disgusted with life's misery and brevity. He even was distracted by his "friends" whose comfort did not bring ease but more trouble and more unanswered questions (see Job 16:2 ff.).

Our trials can make us or break us. They can turn us away from God or turn us to Him. It is hard to turn to Him when it seems as if He has turned away from us. It is especially difficult, in a world that encourages us to defend ourselves, asking "What did I do to deserve this?," to rely on the Great Defender Himself. When we are victims, Christ says we are victors, if we rely on the promise that even when it may seem as if He has forsaken us, He never did and never will. (Proverbs 3:5, 6; Hebrews 13:5). Although this world can falsely manipulate us to believe that "I must have done something wrong" or that "God must be punishing me," God's Word tells us just the opposite, as Jesus was willingly separated from God in order for us to be spiritually reunited with Him. Jesus is our bridge over troubled waters.

We may never have the answers to all of our questions, but Christ will always have the right question for all of His answers. Will you trust Me with your life, even in the midst of death?

In both Job, and Psalm 22, no categorical answer is given which, when handed to every sufferer, will silence all questions. But, for Christ-followers, an answer is given. The answer is found in God's revelation of Himself to Job (Job 38 through 42), to David (Psalm 22:4-6, 9-11, 22-31) and to us (Matthew 27:46). In His divine disclosure, we find the only adequate answer for anybody facing excruciating and inscrutable suffering: fellowship with God. This fellowship so refreshed Job's faith, and David's hope, that they were content to rest their cases with God and raise no further questions or concerns. *Thy will be done!* And although, as children of God, we must each travel our own trail of suffering (be it physical, emotional, and/or spiritual), the way is not unmarked, as Jesus, our Great High Priest, who can truly empathize with us (Hebrews 4:14-16), has blazed that trail beyond anything we could have experienced ourselves. The King of Kings and Lord of Lords allowed Himself to be *forsaken*, so that those of us who believe in Him will not only be *forgiven* (Acts 10:43), but will never be *forgotten* (Luke 12:6, 7), as God keeps His promises to us. It is no wonder that YHWH, the personal and covenant name of God, occurs in Psalm 22 seven (the number of completion) times! He is reminding us that He is personally concerned about our suffering, and that He will keep his promise to never leave us or forsake us in the midst of them. In these truths, we can find hope even in the midst of hopelessness.

HOW CAN A LOVING GOD TORTURE PEOPLE IN HELL?

"Do not be afraid of those who kill the body but cannot kill the soul. Rather, be afraid of the One who can destroy both soul and body in hell."

Matthew 10:28

A quick answer to the above question may go like this: God is not only "love," but also "light, and in Him there is no darkness at all" (1 John 1:5). A holy God could never tolerate the presence of sin. But it is not only sin which results in human beings being cast into hell. It is more directly their attitude toward God's Son that gets them there. In view of the fact that the infinite God who created us gave His Son to be our Savior, the greatest insult and act of rebellion against God that human beings could ever commit is to reject this "unspeakable gift" (2 Corinthians 9:15). When a person does so, there is no need to "justify" God in allowing such a person to enter hell.

Listen to what Jonathan Edwards, the prominent preacher of the "Great Awakening" in the colonial days of Connecticut, considered by historians to have been the "most intelligent and greatest mind America ever produced," had to say: "It is no security to wicked men for one moment, that there are no visible means of death at hand. It is no security to a natural man, that he is now in health, and that he does not see which way he should now immediately go out of the world by any accident, and that there is no visible danger in any respect in his circumstances. The manifold and continual experiences of the world in all ages show there is no evidence that a man is not on the very brink of eternity, and that the next step will not be into another world. The unseen, unthought of ways and means of persons going suddenly out of the world are innumerable and inconceivable. Unconverted persons walk over the pit of hell on a rotten covering, and there are innumerable places in this covering so weak that they will not bear their weight, and these places are not seen. Natural men's prudence and care to preserve their own lives, or the care of others to preserve them, do not secure them for one moment."

What was true in the first century in Jerusalem, and in the eighteenth century in New England, is true today. To refuse to acknowledge such things as sin (Romans 3:23), atonement (John 3:16, 17), hell (John 3:36; 2 Thessalonians 1:5, 8-9), etc., is like a criminal refusing to accept the penalties of the laws of the land. He may reject the laws, but he suffers the penalty just the same. The Good News is that we don't have to, if we admit our need for forgiveness, accept Christ's punishment for our sins, and live by the Spirit of life who saves us from death, not only temporally, but eternally (Romans 6:23).

In view of the uncertainty of life, it is well to keep in mind the words of 2 Corinthians 6:2: "Behold, now is the accepted time: behold, now is the day of salvation." This implies that whenever we are made conscious, by any means, of our need for salvation, it is God's time for us to come to Him through faith in Christ (Ephesians 2:8, 9). We have no assurance that there will be another opportunity.

HOW CAN I BELIEVE IN A LOVING GOD WHEN SUFFERING AND EVIL ABOUND?

"...in the day that you eat of it, you will surely die."

Genesis 2:17b

From a Christian perspective, the risks involved in creation were not only for human beings. God Himself risked a lot in creating the world. The Scriptural perspective reveals a God who throughout the history of the world suffered from the bad choices that human beings made. He suffers because He loves.

In Genesis, we read about God giving Adam and Eve a "menu" of fruits available on the trees of the Garden of Eden. Yet, there was one tree whose fruit Adam and Eve were warned not to eat. If they ate of it, they would die, not only physically, but emotionally and spiritually in an eternity separated from God.

In the Book of Hosea, God portrays Himself as one who is married to and faithfully loving towards a wife who will not be faithful to Him. She not only harms herself, her husband, and her children by becoming a prostitute, but also refuses to acknowledge her sins and her failures as a wife. Yet, He never leaves her or forsakes her. In the same way, while filled with pain, God attempts to call His people, His bride, back to a faithful relationship with Him. But who would want a bride that is only His bride by force rather than choice? And the church is called the Bride of Christ.

The creation was so risky for God, according to the Bible, that it involved Him in becoming human and dying a hellish death on the cross on our behalf (Romans 6:23). Even in the midst of all of our rebellion against God, He loved us so much that He was willing to go to this extreme to have a relationship with us. On the cross, He took upon Himself all the sin of the world, along with all the suffering and evil it produces. He didn't have to do so. He did it out of love for us, because we matter to Him, and because, in God's eyes, you are worth dying for (John 3:16, 17)!

If this short life is all there is and if the suffering death of victims was the "final act" in their role of living on this earth, then we could rightfully say that the risk of creating a world like ours is not worth it. But if what Christ-followers believe is true, then this is simply not the case. As Henri Nouwen, one of my "heroes" whom I had the pleasure of meeting put it, "Life is but a brief interruption of eternity." And our earthly, temporary lives are nothing but a brief prelude to a life that will continue forever. Even though, for many people, this life is filled with nothing but pain and suffering, from an eternal perspective, what they are experiencing is only one little part of the whole plot of the story that God has created for us. Jesus died on the cross so that human beings could live eternally in the peace and joy of God's presence. According to Scripture, that state of being will be such that our present sufferings can't even compare to it in greatness (Romans 8:18, 1 Cor. 2:9)!

When we reflect upon Auschwitz, Vietnam, terrorist attacks, and other evil events of history, heaven must be incomprehensibly wonderful-which is exactly what the Bible tells us!

If there's no heaven, then all the suffering and sickness of dying children, innocent victims, and loving family members is truly meaningless. Death would be tragic and final for all of us. Thankfully, we know better, as Jesus Christ triumphed over death and will empower you to do the same, not only today, but also for eternity, as you lean on Him rather than yourself (Proverbs 3:5,6; 1 Cor. 15:26).

HOW CAN SOMEBODY ELSE'S DEATH PARDON ME?

"...He himself bore our sins in his body on the tree,
so that we might die to sins and live for righteousness;
by his wounds you have been healed."

1 Peter 2:24

Growing up in the tradition passed on to me by my parents, I was often frustrated about my growth in "goodness and holiness," or lack thereof. Although I would somewhat consistently confess my sins to a priest every Saturday afternoon, doing penance to alleviate, or even remove, my guilt in order to be free to receive communion the next morning, I often found that it wouldn't take long before the cycle of sin began once again in my life-even as early as Sunday morning!

Over the years, the Scripture stating that "...it is impossible for the blood of bulls and goats to take away sins (Hebrews 10:4)" truly resonated with me in my experience. You see, although I never had to sacrifice animals in atonement for my sins, as the Jews of the early years had been instructed to do in making payment for their sins (see Leviticus 5:5-10 as one example), I always felt that the sacrifices I did offer to God got me nowhere. Although there may have been a sense that my sins had been paid for, there was never a true sense that my sinful *ways*, in my thoughts, words, and actions, had been disempowered. And so I learned, as the Apostle Paul reminded the believers in Rome, that "There is no one righteous, not even one...there is no one who does good, not even one... their tongues practice deceit...their mouths are full of cursing and bitterness...all have sinned and fall short of the glory of God (Romans 3)."In a personal way, the cycle of sin, confession, repentance, more sin, confession, and repentance was made real in my life. I learned that things were hopeless until I found the God of hope (Romans 7:24, 25).

I learned that my deliverance could not come through a bunch of good deeds and prayers, or, as the Israelites may have learned, through a bunch of sacrificed *lambs*, but from *The Lamb* of God, who takes away the sins of the world (John 1:29).

When Jesus died on the cross for our sins, he provided not only *payment* for our sins (Romans 6:23), but also *power* to overcome them (Romans 6:1-4). This is truly Good News (a.k.a. "Gospel")! In the days of the Old Covenant, or Old Testament, Jeremiah prophesied about a New Covenant, or New Testament, that the Lord would make. As we read, "The time is coming, declares the Lord, when I will make a new covenant with the house of Israel and with the house of Judah. It will not be like the covenant I made with their forefathers, when I took them out of Egypt, because they broke my covenant, though I was a husband to them, declares the Lord. This is the covenant I will make with the house of Israel after that time, declares the Lord. I will put my law in their *minds* and write it on their *hearts*. I will be their God and they will be my people...I will forgive their wickedness and remember their sins no more (Jeremiah 31:31-34)." Isaiah tells us that this promise is for *all* people, both Jew and Gentile (Isaiah 42), who rely on the promised Messiah, rather than on themselves, for deliverance from guilt.

The basic theme: The blood of lambs provided payment of sins, but never power to overcome our sinful nature, which only the blood of The Lamb, Christ Jesus, could do! And what did it take? It took God providing a means by which our very nature would be changed, a means by which we would no longer be judged by the external observance of the law, but rather by the internal acceptance of the Lord, whose Spirit changes our very hearts and minds!

The Apostle Paul said, "If anyone is in Christ he is a new creation, the old is gone and the new has come (2 Corinthians 5:17)." Are you a new creation? If not, why not? Are you still hanging on to the "old," even though you are part of what's new (Romans 6:5-7)? Join me in moving on in a relationship, rather than a religion, with God through Christ based not upon our performance, but rather our reliance, on the One who can truly set us free (John 8:32).

JUST LIKE JESUS

Thomas a Kempis, a fifteenth century monk, had the following to share:

He who follows Me, says Christ our Saviour, walks not in darkness, for he will have the light of life. These are the words of our Lord Jesus Christ, and by them we are admonished to follow His teachings and His manner of living, if we would truly be enlightened and delivered from all blindness of heart.

Let all the study of our heart be from now on to have our meditation fixed wholly on the life of Christ, for His holy teachings are of more virtue and strength than the words of all the angels and saints. And he who through grace has the inner eye of his soul opened to the true beholding of the Gospels of Christ will find in them hidden manna.

It is often seen that those who hear the Gospels find little sweetness in them; the reason is that they do not have the spirit of Christ.

As this fifteenth century monk explained, we cannot become more like Jesus without having the Spirit of Jesus within us. For this reason, we humbly receive God's grace by acknowledging our need for forgiveness, turning from our sins, and turning to Christ who paid for our sins on the cross. This is how we are justified before God (see John 3:16, Romans 1:17, Ephesians 2:8, 9).

Although we are *justified*, or "made right in God's eyes" by our *faith* in Christ, we are called to be *sanctified*, or "made holy" through our *walk* with Him. Yet, we cannot *walk* with Him without being "in *step* with the Spirit (Galatians 5:25)." That is why we are called to cultivate the fruit of the Spirit, in order to become more like Jesus, who embodied the Holy Spirit in all fullness.

On a scale of one to ten (one meaning "I *really* need to grow in Christ-likeness" and ten meaning "I'm cultivating the fruit daily"), how would you rate yourself? How might those closest to you rate you? Why? What can you do to grow through cultivating the fruit of the Spirit this week?

TRUE LOVE

"I just don't love him/her anymore." "We are different people than we were when we got married, and we've fallen out of love." "My feelings towards my husband/wife have changed so much, that I wonder if I've married the wrong person-maybe I made a mistake." "We shared similar expectations, hopes, and dreams-but now all of that has changed, as the feelings just aren't there any more." "I used to wonder how I could ever live without (fill in name), but now I wonder how I can live with him/her."

"My parents never loved me, so how can I love them?" "He/she doesn't treat me very well, so why should I treat him/her any differently?" "I was always jealous of my brother/sister, so it's good enough that I am no longer jealous of him/her-but I wouldn't say that I actually love him/her. How could I? Wouldn't that be foolish?"

"I can't stand to be around so and so at work." "I used to like him/her, but then he/she hurt me."

During counseling opportunities, I am quite often asked what a married couple should do when they are no longer "in love." Likewise, I am asked by others how they should respond to someone they do not "love." My answer is always the same: *Learn* how to love each other. Although this answer may at first seem *simplistic*, it is the only answer that is *realistic*, as we find it in God's Word. "You have heard that it was said, 'Love your friends and hate your enemies. But I tell you: Love your enemies and pray for those who persecute you, that you may prove to be children of your Father in heaven (Matthew 5:43-45a)." How could Jesus say such a thing? He knew the source of love was not from within us, but from God.

Contrary to popular opinion, love is not primarily a *feeling* but an *action*. And love is not equivalent to lust, despite the suggestions from advertisers. In fact, many have said that the opposite of "love" is not "hate," but "lust," as lust "can't wait" to meet its own selfish needs, whereas love always waits, being patient while putting the needs of another above its own needs.

In 1 Corinthians 13:4-8, the Apostle Paul gives us a definition of true love. Interestingly enough, only Greek *verbal* forms are used to describe true love. These verbal forms reveal an internal attitude, rather than an external behavior, that is indicative of love. Nowhere in the text can one find a definition of love that is emotive. What does this mean? It means that love is something that we can choose to offer others, whether or not we "feel" like it. If we wait until we "feel" like acting lovingly towards a particular person or persons in our lives, we may be waiting for a very long time. If, on the other hand, we choose to *act* in love, treating another person the way that we would want him/her to treat us (Matthew 7:12), regardless of whether or not they reciprocate, we will show those around us (including the "unlovable") that we are children of God. Often times the "feelings" of love will follow, even romantic feelings, when appropriate.

The Song of Solomon, chapter one, describes some of the feelings that a couple in a monogamous relationship, based on trust and free from fear, could experience. Yet, even without such feelings, we are called by God to love others, especially our spouses, the way that He loves us. "But God demonstrated his own love for us in this: While we were still sinners, Christ died for us (Romans 5:8)." While we were very "unlovable," before we even realized our need for Him, even when we were "ugly" from a spiritual, relational, or emotional viewpoint, rejecting the truth that we now accept, Christ Jesus died for us.

Who will you die for? Jesus said that we cannot be His disciples unless we put our selfish wishes and desires on our cross (Mark 8:34), and follow Him, loving others the way that He loves us. This is impossible without His help. The Good News is that we are not left alone to try to love others this way through our own human, natural abilities. We have been offered a superhuman, supernatural ability through the love and forgiveness of Jesus Christ and the presence of God's Spirit in our lives. "We love because He first loved us (1 John 4:19)."

Have you received His love? If not, why not? I believe that the extent to which we are able to love others is directly proportionate to the extent to which we've received God's love. Will you receive God's love, even for those aspects of yourself that you see as "unlovable?"You are loved with an everlasting love (Jeremiah 31:3)!

PASSIONATE PATIENCE

It is often amazing to see the measure of God's patience as compared to our own level of patience. It is also rewarding to recognize the example of perseverance that we see in others who have inspired us to "never give up." So many stories flood my mind when I think of perseverance through the trials of life, whether circumstantial or relational. To name just a few, I think of political leaders like Abraham Lincoln, Winston Churchill, and Mahatma Ghandi; industry leaders like Johannes Gutenberg, or more recently, Steve Jobs, and spiritual leaders like Martin Luther, Richard Wermbrandt, and Jonathan Edwards.

Scripture also has a long list of names of those who persevered through thick and thin, enduring hardships and enduring the people who made things hard. In Hebrews chapter 11, we read about the many heroes of the faith who never lost sight of God's presence, power, protection, peace, and even His patience with them and others. Near the end of the chapter, we read a little bit about the "rewards" for persevering that some of these servants of God received: "… (those) who conquered kingdoms, administered justice, and gained what was promised; who shut the mouths of lions, quenched the fury of flames, and escaped the edge of the sword; whose weakness was turned to strength; and who became powerful in battle and routed foreign armies. Women received back their dead, raised to life again (Hebrews 11:33-35a)."

I can easily welcome the rewards mentioned above. However, it is the second part of verse 35 and what follows that I am sometimes tempted to overlook: "Others were tortured and refused to be released, so that they might gain a better resurrection. Some faced jeers and flogging, while still others were chained and put into prison. They were stoned; they were sawed in two; they were put to death by the sword. They went about in sheepskins and goatskins, destitute, persecuted and mistreated-the world was not worthy of them... These were all commended for their faith, yet none of them received what had been promised. God had planned something better for us so that only together with us would they be made perfect (Hebrews 11:35b-39)."

In my own human limitations, I would much rather receive the first set of rewards mentioned above (i.e. conquering kingdoms, escaping the edge of the sword, etc.) than the second set of "rewards (i.e. persecution, torture, and death)." Yet both sets of believers, those who experienced "good times" on this earth, and those who experienced one tragedy after another, are *equally* commended for their faith (vs. 39). We so often are tempted to believe that our trials with various circumstances of life and with various people in our lives are proof that God does *not* love us. What a lie of the enemy we are tempted to believe when the going gets rough, or when others become tough (at least tough to deal with). Yet, the very opposite is true-nothing can separate us from the love of God that is in Christ Jesus our Lord (Romans 8:35-39)!

So why does God sometimes allow us to experience all kinds of hardships with others and with ourselves? There are lots of reasons, many of which we could never even fathom.

But perhaps one reason is this: God wants to make us more like His Son (Romans 8:29). Part of becoming more like Jesus involves developing the type of patience and perseverance that He had displayed right up until the time He said "It is finished (John 19:30)." Regarding Jesus, Scripture also tells us that "Although he was a son, he learned obedience from what he *suffered* and, once made perfect, he became the source of eternal salvation for all who obey him...(Hebrews 5:8,9)."

Jesus accomplished what He came to the earth to do. How did He do it? He did it not only by developing endurance, but also by embracing suffering. Patience deals with enduring. Passion deals with suffering. Patience and Passion are two sides to the same coin of God's love, which is most vividly demonstrated in the cross of Christ. God could have wiped us all away. Instead, He gave us another chance, as He patiently waits for us to become more like the One in whose image we are created. Once we are "there," we will have true fulfillment and contentment in life. He died for us so that we could live not only abundantly (in its true sense), but also eternally. The cross of Christ not only demonstrates the most profound statement of God's love, but also the most profound statement of God's suffering, for without His captivity, we would never have our freedom.

Are you willing to take up your cross, placing on it the need to be in control as you allow God to be in control of your life. Are you willing to be patient with others, as God has been patient with you? How long has God waited for you to allow Him to be not only your Savior, but also your Lord, when it comes to your response to difficult situations and people? How long has Jesus waited for you to change your attitude and actions, being free from what keeps you from experiencing the truly "good life," while loving you all of the way? If God can wait many years for us, we can certainly be willing to wait a few years for others, and in so doing, become more Christ-like as a result.

FAITHFULNESS

How well do you "measure up" to the faith that God desires for us to have? When the going gets tough, do you still keep going, or do you give up? When it seems as though God's promises come true for everybody else, but not for you, do you lose hope? Do you trust God to fulfill His promises, or do you doubt God and the promises He gives you? Available in our church library is a book you may have seen before entitled God's Promises for Your Every Need, by Word Publishing. In it, Dr. A.L. Gill compiles scriptures relating to eighty promises from God to you, based on hundreds of verses of God's Word. I am sure there are many more promises than that. However, let's consider just one of the promises listed on page 180 of that book:

"I tell you the truth, if you have *faith* as small as a mustard seed, you can say to this mountain, 'Move from here to there' and it will move. *Nothing* will be impossible for you" (Matthew 17:20-21). Through interpreting this verse in the context of the entire Bible, we realize that nothing is impossible, so long as it is within God's plan for you, the plan that will bring you the most contentment and joy in the long run (Romans 8:28,29). That is what Jesus is telling us.

If our faith is based on something other than Jesus (i.e. ourselves, other human beings, our power, prestige, position, external qualities, educational, professional or financial accomplishments, or the faith of someone else), then our faith is *smaller* than a mustard seed.

The mustard seed was the smallest of garden seeds known in that day (orchard seeds, though smaller, were unknown in that part of the world). Jesus' point was not that we need "more faith," in a quantitative way, in order to receive His promises. (Some teach the false doctrine of believing that if we just have "more faith" we could raise the dead, ride in a Rolls Royce, and receive the riches of this world. As a result, if you die from having cancer, and are later buried, it's your fault that you weren't healed, as you didn't have "enough" faith. Besides inflicting cruelty upon others, such false doctrine puts us on the throne of our lives and our destinies, rather than God).

Jesus made it clear that the question we must ask ourselves, when it comes to our faith, is not whether or not we have *enough* faith, as the tiniest amount of faith, the faith of a mustard seed, could move mountains. Instead, we ask ourselves what we have faith *in*-what is the *object* of our faith.

If the object of our faith is Jesus Christ, then "quantity" doesn't matter, as "one size fits all." But if the object of our faith is something or someone other than Jesus, then we will never have enough faith to do the things that we need to do in this life, or to receive the blessings that God promises us as members of His family. So the question is not "How much faith do I have," but "Do I have faith in the right thing(s)?" Therefore, we become more concerned with the type of faith we have, whether it is the type of faith Abraham had, believing God without doubt despite the circumstances in his life, or the type of faith that Jesus' disciples had when they were more concerned about casting out demons than glorifying Christ (see Matthew 17:14-20). What is your faith based upon? Where is your faith? Is it in Christ, or is it misplaced?

FIRM BUT GENTLE

"Then neither do I condemn you," Jesus declared.
"Go now and leave your life of sin."

John 8:11

When we reflect upon the response Jesus demonstrated regarding the woman caught in adultery, as written in John 8:1-11, we cannot help but see Jesus' gentleness in dealing with the situation at hand. Rather than condemning this woman, a verdict that her accusers were more than happy to carry out, Jesus releases her from judgment.

The incident was staged to trap Jesus (vs. 6). Even though under Jewish law execution by stoning had only been prescribed for engaged virgins and the men who slept with them (Deuteronomy 22:23-24), the woman's accusers had altered the law to fit their own agenda. They wanted badly to accuse Jesus. The Romans didn't allow the Jews to carry out death sentences (see John 18:31). Therefore, if Jesus had ordered them to stone her, he could have been in conflict with the Romans. If he had ordered them not to stone her, he could have been accused of ignoring the law.

Jesus, in His infinite wisdom, disarmed the accusers. Because he spoke of throwing a stone, He could not be accused of failing to obey the law. But the qualification for throwing a stone prevented anyone from acting. When Jesus said, *"If any* one of you is without sin, let him be the first to throw a stone at her (8:7)," the words "without sin" meant "without ANY sin," not just sexual sin. What wisdom our Lord has! Because the men were either convicted in their hearts or afraid of what might happen to them if they lied, they ALL left!

Notice two things. First, Jesus did not harshly rebuke the accusers who acted in self-righteousness and arrogance, but rather enabled them to realize their own guilt in the situation. He could have told them all the right answers, but instead He asked them the right questions, as any humble and effective leader would do. He was gentle with them. Second, Jesus did not tell the woman, after her accusers had left, that she "owed Him one." Rather, he loved her enough to tell her what she *needed* to hear, whether or not it was what she *wanted* to hear, as he responded *"Go and sin no more."* Jesus was not only gentle with her, but He was firm with her sinfulness. Jesus' type of gentleness enables others to receive the firmness of a correction, or a confrontation, in a way that shows their understanding of the motivation for His firmness: His love.

If we are always gentle and never firm, we are no more effective in bringing about life-change in others than some popular talk show hosts known for their "tolerance" of all people and all behavior. However, if we are always firm and never gentle, we run the risks of becoming judges with no jury, leaders without followers, and Christians without Christ. Jesus strikes the balance between the two. Let us follow Him in being firm, but gentle, in regard to the truth that can set us all free (John 8:32).

JESUS THE ONE AND ONLY

A Devotional based on John 10:22-39

After years of seeking an answer to the question of "What happens when we die?," I finally "saw the light." As an Accounting major in undergraduate school, there were only so many "philosophy" or "comparative religion" classes in which I could enroll. Because the questions I began asking as a child were heavy on my heart as a young adult, I registered for as many of these courses as I could.

The time was prime for me to find an answer to one of life's largest questions. My father had experienced his first heart-attack, my "adopted grandmother" had undergone a stroke, and one of my closest friends in my fraternity house had been killed in a drunk-driving car accident. At a time in my life in which it seemed as if unconditional love was hard to find anywhere, I found it in my sister Elizabeth, a devout Christ-follower who lived 4,000 miles away where she attended graduate school. It seemed as if Liz sent me a new Bible every Christmas. Yet, I never cracked a Bible open until that intentionally decisive year in which I was confronted with the question of "What happens when we die?" in a new way. And when I did, I was amazed at what I found.

Mohammed, Buddha, Confucious and other spiritual leaders never claimed to be God. No wonder people are not easily offended by them. Yet, Jesus did. He claimed to be "God in the flesh," one with the Father (John 10:30), and the only way to eternal life (John 14:6). One other truth that hit me hard that year: The spiritual leaders of the "religious movements" of the ages were all in their graves. Jesus wasn't, nor is He today. All of the historical evidence one can find supports the truth that Jesus rose from the dead. As a result, I realized that Jesus, who overcame death, could help me do the same so that I would not have to fear death, and would be free to live. I needed simply to cry out to Him (Romans 10:9-13).

I believe that those who are most prepared to die are best prepared to live. Even in my depressed, suicidal state of mind at the time, I began to have hope in the One who could possibly show me the way out of the darkness and into His light, as Jesus is the light of the world (Isaiah 9:2, 53:11, 60:1, 19; John 8:12, etc.). He changed my life, and He can change yours too. Yet, without him, you will never be able to live the life you were created to live, as He is the author of life (Colossians 1:15-22) who created you to live it.

Is Christ your savior? If so, is He also your leader, or "Lord?" Christ is not Lord at all unless He is Lord of all. Open your heart to Him, and you will never be disappointed, nor will you ever *want* to die, as you will have a reason to live (John 5:24).

LOST AND FOUND

A Devotional based on Luke 15:11-31

Sometimes those of us who think we have been "found" are more lost than we ever imagined. We might have all the right answers but ask all the wrong questions. Perhaps this is why Jesus tells a parable about a lost "younger" son, but includes his older son in it. The younger son's sin was blatant, and evident to everyone. But eventually, the younger son's sin led to sorrow and surrender to the son's father.

On the other hand, the older son, who might have thought he was not as "lost" as his younger (or "less mature") brother, responded to the younger son's repentance with ridicule rather than rejoicing. Why? Perhaps he did everything "right" for such a long time, and envied his younger brother who was being celebrated even after doing everything wrong. And so what does he do? He tells his father how things should be handled (vv. 29-30). In other words, he's giving answers without asking questions. But if he asked questions, what would have been good for him to ask? He could have asked his father why he had so much joy over the younger son's return. He could have asked his father how he could cause him to rejoice. He could have learned that when it came to pleasing his father, what he did externally by doing all the "right" things, did not matter in comparison to what he thought and felt internally by having the wrong heart. The same is true in our relationship to our

Father in heaven, and to His "younger," or "less right-living" children.

In God the Father's eyes, our external behavior means nothing in light of our internal attitude. "For God does not see as man sees. For man looks at external qualities, but God looks at the heart" (1 Samuel 16:7). King David learned this lesson well. He realized the depths of his own sinful nature, admitting that he was sinful at birth (Psalm 51:5) and that he was no better later in his life, dependent upon God's grace alone for "cleansing" (vv. 7-9). David realized, perhaps the hard way, that God does not delight in "right" behavior, but in a broken and contrite heart, a humble heart that is not self-righteous but softened by the touch of God (vv. 16,17) and the needs of others (vs. 18). Only that type of heart can lead to healing and hope in our lives and the lives of those we serve. Only that type of heart can lead to handling all of life in a way that connects how we think and how we feel to how we behave and how we live. Only then can we be "found" to be whole, with our heads, hearts, and hands all working together as an integrated whole.

The older son's hand (his behavior) was not connected to his heart (the way he was thinking). What you saw was not what you got. Sure, he behaved right, and had the "right" way of living. Yet, he did not have the right heart. He did not obey God's truth that we can do everything right, but be wrong, because our motives are not right (1 Corinthians 13). If our hearts are in the wrong place, regardless of where our bodies are, we are still lost. If our hearts are in the right place, then there's hope that we will truly be found.

LOVE HAS GOOD MANNERS

"It is not rude, it is not self-seeking, it is not easily angered, it keeps no record of wrongs."

1 Corinthians 13:5

Jesus shows us what the above definition of love looks like in person. From reading John 8:3-11, we see many facets of the fact that love has good manners. First, love is not rude. The teachers of the law and the Pharisees were being rude when they brought this woman, caught in adultery, to stand before a crowd and before Jesus, most likely against her own will. They had no consideration for her personal dignity (vs. 3), totally disrespecting her as a person created in God's image (Gen. 1:27), putting her on the spot and exposing her shame to the spotlight (vs. 3b). Jesus, on the other hand, didn't look at her but instead looked down, where he wrote upon the ground (vs. 6b). Jesus did not act unbecomingly, even toward someone whose life may have been unbecoming.

Second, love is not self-seeking. Unlike the Pharisees who sought attention for themselves from amongst the crowds who were paying attention to Jesus (vs. 2), Jesus did not exalt Himself. His desire to lead the people was not for His own sake but for theirs. Perhaps that is why He "sat" down (vs. 2) before all the people, whereas the Pharisees stood (vs. 3) proudly and arrogantly. Even Jesus' posture in this scene was one of humility rather than pride, other-seeking rather than self-seeking.

Third, love is not easily angered. People who are not easily angered usually do not start lawsuits (as opposed to those in Corinth to whom Paul would later write-see 1 Cor. 6:1-11). And that is exactly what the teachers of the law were doing, as they brought this woman to Jesus with hopes of accusing Jesus of breaking the law (vv. 4-6). On the other hand, Jesus had every right to be very angry with the teachers of the law. Yet, instead of allowing them to "get the best of Him," He sought the best from them by giving them the best of answers, saying, "If any one of you is without sin, let him be the first to throw a stone at her (vs. 7)." The rest is history.

Finally, love keeps no record of wrongs. The woman's accusers kept lots of records. They gladly pointed out her errors. On the other hand, Jesus, who knew all of their sins, decided not to list hers. Instead, when everyone else had left, he faced her, asking, "Woman, where are they? Has no one condemned you?" To which she responded, "No one, sir." She addressed him with respect, as He had shown respect Himself. Best of all, He kept no record of her wrongs. He had every right to do so. Yet, through His forgiveness, her sins would be forgotten, if her old life was forsaken (vs. 11). Because of His love, she could lose her life in order to gain His life (Matthew 16:25) so that she could live her life free from condemnation, accusation, and tribulation, and so can we.

When it comes to the "good manners" of love, are you more like the teachers of the law or the Lord? What will you do to be in line with Jesus' life and His love?

TRAVELLING COMPANIONS

"Where I am going, you cannot follow now, but you will follow later...Thomas said to him, 'Lord, we don't know where you are going, so how can we know the way?' Jesus answered, 'I am the way and the truth and the life. No one comes to the Father except through me.' "

John 13:36b-14:6

No matter where we are heading on any type of journey, the *means* does not justify the *ends*. "Getting there" does not justify *how* we got there, especially when we traveled in a way that was not consistent with God's Word and the leading of His Spirit in our lives.

The only "map" that Jesus gave His first disciples was Himself. "I am the way... (John 14:6)." We have not only Jesus, the "Living Word, but also the Bible, the "Written Word," as our guide. Any other way we take, both in our public and private lives, is nothing but a shortcut.

In my small group's meeting one night, a certain member of the group mentioned that our "short-cuts" often prove to be anything but. My wife gracefully nudged me, reminding me that my short-cuts are *never* the shortest distance between two points!

In 1 Samuel 26, we read about King David, who could have taken a short-cut on his way to the royal throne of Israel.

His enemy, Saul, motivated by jealousy, hunted him down like an animal. Saul knew that the Lord was lifting up David as the next leader of Israel, a godly leader who would truly shepherd the sheep. At one point in the story, Saul, who had been trying to kill David, was within inches of the possibility of being killed himself. The Lord allowed Saul to be at David's hand, as we read the words of Abishai, David's servant, speaking to David: "Today God has delivered your enemy into your hands. Now let me pin him to the ground with one thrust of my spear; I won't strike him twice (1 Samuel 26:9-11)."

Abishai was the one man who answered the question "Who will go…with me to Saul?" (1 Samuel 26:6) affirmatively. However, Abishai had a different attitude than that of David. Unlike Abishai, and many of us, David refused to repay evil with evil. Instead, in his Christ-likeness, he overcame evil with goodness, just as we are exhorted to do (Romans 12:21). After all, David knew that the Lord was preparing him to be the next leader of Israel, as he had earlier been anointed by Samuel (see 1 Samuel 16). David could have taken a short-"cut" to the throne, by *cutting* Saul's life with a spear. Instead, he entrusted Saul, whom he respectfully called the "Lord's Anointed (vs. 9)," to God who asks us all to leave our lives, and circumstances in His hands. Although Saul had attempted to kill David many times, David refused the opportunity to do the same, believing that God would not only protect him from Saul, but would also reward him for traveling on the journey to the throne in a *supernatural*, rather than natural, way. David prayed for his enemy and entrusted himself to God for protection and for the right timing at which David would be seated on the throne of Israel.

David could have traveled by the way of selfishness. Instead, he chose the way of selflessness. He could have taken the way of self-promotion. Instead, he chose the way of humiliation. The Lord tells us that "Whoever exalts himself will be humbled, and whoever humbles himself will be exalted (Matthew 23:12)." Paul tells us that our attitude should be that of Christ Jesus, who humbled Himself in every way, and was rewarded in the long-term (Philippians 2:5-11).

As you travel your journey with the Lord and even with other believers, which way are you choosing to travel? Jesus said "*I am the way.*" In your work, in your home, and in our community, are you moving up by knocking other people down? Are you climbing the proverbial "ladder" only by stepping on other people's heads? Are you using your authority to lord it over others, or to serve them (Luke 22:25-27)? *How* we get to the finish line of our journey is just as important as whether or not we get there. When God wills the ends, He also wills the means. The way we travel will affect the results of our journey when we cross that finish line. Will you travel by the ways of this world or by Jesus' way, the way of humility, submission, and forgiveness? Only by doing things Jesus' way will we be able to see the vision which He has cast for us.

KNOWING WHERE YOU'RE GOING

"And we know that in all things God works for the good of those who love him, who have been called according to his purpose. For those God foreknew he also predestined to be conformed to the likeness of his Son..."

Romans 8:28-29a

Many of us love to quote Romans 8:28, don't we? Even when someone we know has experienced horrendous pain and suffering, and we would do best to keep our mouths shut and our ears open, we can be quick to say that "Everything happens for a reason...God has a plan in all of this...Just have faith," etc., ad nausea. Much of this "help" that we are tempted to offer often comes with good intentions. We want to comfort others, bringing some type of peace to their anxieties. These are not evil motives. On the other hand, sometimes we can slip into the mistake of telling ourselves that "everything happens for a reason," without realizing the context in which the Apostle Paul made that statement. It is sad that the ultimate purpose for which God sometimes allows us to experience "all kinds of trials" (James 1:2) is completely lost in a litany of well-meaning words offered to someone who may be finding anything but "joy" (James 1:2) in the midst of their trials.

So what is that "ultimate purpose?" The ultimate purpose is not found in Romans 8:28, quoted and misquoted again and again. We find it in the often overlooked words of Romans

8:29. The ultimate purpose of everything that God allows into our lives (emotionally, physically, financially, spiritually-to name just a few) is to *conform us to the "likeness of his Son."* What does that mean? Does that mean we will become less conformed to the ways of this world as we are transformed by the renewing of our minds (Romans 12:2)? Does it mean that we will experience true contentment in life as we let the peace of God rule in our hearts (Colossians 3:15)? Does it mean that we will experience victory over death (1 Corinthians 15:54), power over evil (Romans 16:20), and healing of our infirmities (Luke 10:9)? Yes, it includes all of these things that we often gain through Bible Study, Prayer, and Fellowship. But it also includes something else.

Could we describe the Christian life as including joy? Sometimes. Could we describe the Christian life as being peaceful? Sometimes. Should we describe it as being victorious? We could. Yet, perhaps the best way to describe the Christian life is to describe it as one that is adventurous. Why? Because sometimes the adventure does not always include things that make us feel very joyful, peaceful, or victorious-at least not on the surface. Sometimes it includes pain, persecution, and peril. Sometimes it includes sadness, sorrow, and suffering. Yet without those things, we cannot be "conformed to the image of Christ." Without those things, we cannot become "mature," in Christ, not lacking anything we truly need, whether or not it's what we want (James 1:4).

What is your destination? Where are you heading? At what are you aiming? If you aim at nothing, you'll hit it every time. However, if your aim is to become more like Christ, a goal that can bring you true contentment, fulfillment, and peace inwardly despite what takes place outwardly around you, then you'll have to be willing to suffer, as Christ has suffered for you. As the Apostle James says, "Blessed is the one who perseveres under trial, because when he has stood the test, he will receive the crown of life that God has promised to those who love him (James 1:12)."

Faith is like gold, it stands in the test of fire. Precious metals that melt in fire are not so precious at all. True faith, like true gold, endures no matter how hot the fire gets. The trials and temptations we go through can either make us or break us, refine us or melt us. If we obey the advice of God's Word, we will be refined through the fire, like gold. If not, we will melt like pyrite.

KNOWING WHAT YOU'RE DOING

"Moses said to the LORD, 'O LORD, I have never been eloquent, neither in the past nor since you have spoken to your servant. I am slow of speech and tongue.'"

Exodus 4:10

When it comes to doing our share of God's work, we all can come up with some pretty good excuses of why God may need to ask someone else to do what He's calling us to do. Some reasons why we decline a challenge may stem from our lack of confidence not only in ourselves, but ultimately in God. Many of our "humble" predispositions are not really humble at all. In fact, some forms of "humility" are nothing other than a façade for self-deprecating thoughts about oneself. Yet, there is no room for such thoughts in God's Kingdom.

Moses learned the hard way that when we resist God's desire to bless us through carrying out His work in the lives of others, we often are testing God's patience. Moses' first inhibition, "Who am I, that I should go to Pharaoh...?" (Exodus 3:11) was met by God's grace as He told Moses "I will be with you (3:12)." God wanted Moses to realize that it wasn't his *social position*, but his *spiritual condition*, that would make him effective for God's kingdom. God also wanted Moses to know that He would be *with* him. How amazing that we see Emmanuel, "God with us," with Moses long before Jesus even came to the earth (Isaiah 7:14, 8:8, Matthew 1:23). Yet that was not enough for Moses-as it sometimes is not enough for us!

After Moses asked "Who am I...?", he then asked, "Who are *You* (3:13)?" Again, the LORD answered patiently, "I am who I AM WHO I AM (vs. 14)." Unfortunately, two objections were not enough for Moses. Moses then asked "What if they do not believe me... (Exodus 4:1)?" God then gave him proof to show them that he was sent by God (4:2-9). Was that enough to convince Moses? No. Moses still worried. His fourth concern was his self-perceived inadequacy to do what God was asking him to do, as Moses says, "...O Lord, I have never been eloquent, neither in the past nor since you have spoken to your servant. I am slow of speech and tongue (4:10)." At this point, God reminds Moses of who *He* is, asking, "Who gave man his mouth? Who makes him deaf or mute? Who gives him sight or makes him blind? Is it not I, the LORD? Now go; I will help you speak and will teach you what to say (4:11, 12)."

As if that were not enough encouragement from above, Moses threw in the towel by pleading "O Lord, please send someone else to do it (4:13)." And God did.

We often think of Moses as a "reluctant leader"-and he probably was. Yet, we don't usually think of him as a disobedient servant-which he may have been. When it comes to obeying God, it is not our *performance*, but our *dependence*, that God values. God will use anyone who is willing, even if not able, because He is able. His adequacy more than makes up for our inadequacies. His strength is best displayed through our weakness (2 Corinthians 12:9). And that is why He calls us to follow His leading in our lives in order to make an impact in the lives of others. We cannot do so without being willing to use whatever gift He has given us (1 Peter 4:10) to fulfill our particular role in the body of Christ (1 Cor. 12:12-26).

I once conducted an interview designed to discover the unique giftedness and ministry of an elderly woman in Escondido, California, where I served during seminary as an Associate Pastor of a church plant. This particular woman canceled her appointment with me three times. When we were to first meet, she never arrived for the appointment. In answer to my telephone call, asking "Jill (not actual name), where are you?," she responded "I'm here, but I have no gifts." After reading 1 Peter 4:10, encouraging her to realize that she has at least one gift according to God's Word-and that she is valuable and "usable" in His sight, she agreed to setting up another interview. Again, she didn't show up. After telephoning her, she told me that she didn't want to "waste my time," as there wasn't anything she could possibly be "good at." After explaining that we are all a "10" in some area (1 Cor. 12), she agreed to setting up an appointment a third time. Not being as patient as God was with Moses, I told Jill that I believed in the rules of the old ball game, "Three strikes and you're out!" She showed up. Sure enough, Jill had *many* gifts, and today uses them in ways that nobody else in her church could.

How about you? What are your gifts? Have you taken steps towards discovering them? If not, why not? Are you a reluctant leader or a disobedient servant? Remember, the Lord upholds the lowly but humbles the proud. At the same time, the Lord has a plan for your church and this world, a plan that cannot be fulfilled without you. Will you jump in, letting Him overcome your inadequacies with His sufficiency?

COUNTING THE COST

"Lord, Martha said to Jesus, 'If you had been
here, my brother would not have died.' "

John 11:21

Imagine having a friend, neighbor, or family member who does not yet know the Lord? Imagine that you've prayed for that person's salvation over and over again, for years, seemingly to no avail. Then one day, you cross paths with that person who asks you if you are going to a large evangelistic festival that they continue to see promoted on bumper stickers, billboards, and lawn signs. You tell them "yes" and ask "Would you like to join me?" Much to your surprise and delight, they respond in the affirmative.

When the day of the large event arrives, your friend is ready and waiting. You pick up your friend to drive to the event together. There's only one problem: When you arrive, you are told that the evangelist was not there. A large screen in the front of the auditorium plays a pre-recorded message from the evangelist: His message: "Sorry that I can't be there, but it's the thought that counts."

At this point, your friend begins to wonder what Christians are all about. Are they all hypocrites? Are they all people who promise more than they deliver? Do most of them forget about you when you need them most?

Mary and Martha, two sisters who lived in a town called

Bethany, may have had some of these same thoughts, asking, "Where is He when we need Him most? Our brother is going to die unless He helps us."

Because their brother, Lazarus, was dying, Mary and Martha sent a message requesting Jesus' help, as they were close friends of Jesus and they knew that He loved Lazarus. Jesus did not show up-when they wanted Him to be there, although He did arrive when they needed Him to be there. Mary and Martha knew that it was going to take a power beyond them to save their brother. That power came from Jesus, who, upon arriving at Bethany, saw how grieved Mary and Martha were, and wept (John 11:35).

Jesus demonstrated God's compassion. Then He demonstrated God's power. He showed Mary and Martha that He was not just a "no-show," but that Lazarus was allowed to die in order for others to be drawn to God through a special miracle (John 11:4). He then proceeded to raise their brother from the dead! As a result, many people put their faith in Him (John 11:45), receiving forgiveness of their sins and direction in their lives.

Today, many of us know lots of people, even in our own neighborhoods, workplaces, and homes, who are "dead" in their sins, because they have not yet come to know the Savior. They are held under bondage to their destructive attitudes, thoughts, words, and actions, even when they look as if they "have it altogether" on the surface. Yet, beneath the surface, whether they realize it or not, they are longing for the only One who can meet the needs that they've tried to meet in all the wrong ways. They are crying out for meaning in a meaningless world. They are looking for hope in the midst of hopelessness. They are lacking direction, as they are aiming at nothing, and hitting it every time. They need Jesus.

WHAT HAPPENS NEXT

"Yet a time is coming and has now come when the true worshipers will worship the Father in spirit and truth, for they are the kind of worshipers the Father seeks. God is spirit, and his worshipers must worship in spirit and in truth."

John 4:23

From the beginning of our journey, we have looked to God for guidance. God has amazed us with a strong sense of community, transformation, discovery, and sacrifice. We ask, "Now what?" He is asking us to follow through on our commitments. Then what? What will we do when we "get there," "there" being the point at which the vision the Lord gave us becomes a reality? What will we do when we have our _____? Then, as now, we are called to worship the Master.

The question of *how* to worship God, or *where* to worship Him, is a popular one today. Many of us, perhaps including you, have often struggled with the question of choosing the right "religious" or "spiritual" path towards God. Our society, promoting religious pluralism and social relativism, has not necessarily been very helpful on our quest. Many of us who are Christians have agonized over the decision to choose the right church. Just as the questions of how and where to worship God are popular today, those same questions were asked yesterday, even in the first century, in a culture very similar to that of the twenty-first century. Jesus gave us the answer.

At a time when Jews did whatever it took to *not* pass through Samaria, a land populated by people who were half Jewish and half Gentile, Jesus, the Jew of all Jews, intentionally walked right through it. He stopped at a well and spoke to a woman who had three things going against her in that day and culture: She was a woman (considered "second-class citizens" then). She was a Samaritan (considered "half-breeds," or "social outcasts"). Finally, she was immoral (as she had many "lovers"). Most religious leaders would not touch her with a ten foot pole, then and now. Yet, Jesus was different. He was God in the flesh. He knew what He created this woman to be, and felt sorry about what she had become. He knew how precious she was when she may have felt anything but. He knew she was created in God's image, an image that may be *defaced*, but never *erased*. And so He spoke the truth lovingly to her- and delivered her from her destructive ways as a result.

Jesus came, not for the righteous, but sinners. He came not for the healthy, but the sick (Matthew 9:9-13). And so must we. Are you willing to worship Him by the way you relate to others, both lost and found?

According to God's Word, worshiping in "spirit and in truth" does not depend upon *where* we worship God. The Samaritan woman "reminded" Jesus that the proper place of worship had long been a source of debate between Jews and Samaritans. Samaritans believed that "this mountain" (John 4:19), Mount Gerizim, was sacred. Abraham and Jacob had built altars in the general vicinity (Genesis 12:7; 33:20), and the people were blessed from this mountain (Deut. 11:29; 27:12), rather than

Mount Ebal in Jerusalem, according to the Samaritan Scriptures (which contained only the Pentateuch, the first five books of the Old Testament). Rather, worshiping in "spirit and in truth" depends upon *how* we worship.

The apostle Paul said "...offer your bodies as living sacrifices, holy and pleasing to God-this is your spiritual act of worship. Do not conform any longer to the pattern of this world, but be transformed by the renewing of your mind. Then you will be able to test and approve what God's will is-his good, pleasing, and perfect will (Romans 12:1-2)." In other words, we worship by the way we live our lives.

Today, at each step along our journey with Jesus, let's worship God not only with our words, but also with our actions; not only verbally, but also visually; not only with what we preach, but also with what we practice. Many have said that "actions speak louder than words." I agree. Will you join me in following the One whose actions never contradicted His words, as He is the Living Word? In doing so, we will know Christ and make Him known regardless of the place of our worship, because of the condition of our hearts.

MARRIAGE MATTERS - PRIORITY PRESSURE

"For this reason a man will leave his father and mother and be united to his wife, and they will become one flesh...Therefore what God has joined together, let man not separate."

Matthew 19:5, 6

When you need to make an important decision, where do you go for guidance? When you need to share your thoughts, feelings, and concerns, where do you go to share them? When you are wrestling with issues that are problematic to you, to whom do you turn? When you are feeling down, who lifts you up? When you need comfort, where do you go to find it? When you forget who you are or why you are here, who reminds you? When you finally have free time to spend with another person, who is that person? When you want to just enjoy someone else's company, or share yours with them, who do you choose? Our answers to these and other questions tell us where our hearts are and which relationship we truly value most in our lives.

Whether single, married, divorced, or widowed, God wants us to turn first to Him, so that we can then turn next to the human being who needs to come first in our lives above all other human beings. If we are married, that human being is our spouse, not our children, our parents, our coworkers or even our "best friends."

But what if your spouse makes you miserable? What if you can't stand to be around him or her? What if you are married to someone who seems to be better at knocking you down rather than lifting you up? What if that person abuses you, whether psychologically, emotionally, physically, or sexually? These are tough questions, but God has the answers for you. You see, unless you turn first to Him, you will not be able to turn next to your spouse, as His Word sets the priorities in order. Yet, at the same time, His Word doesn't allow you to subject yourself to abuse, whereby you may be excusing a husband rather than forgiving him, or enabling a wife rather than empowering her.

True "oneness" between a husband and wife cannot be developed when one or both of them are unrepentant of sins that were committed against the other person. If the spouse who is *offended* tries to have reconciliation with the spouse who was *offending* in words, actions, or behavioral patterns, *before* that spouse has repented, then the offended spouse may be confusing forgiving with excusing. As a result, the offending party will not be required to change in his or her attitudes, thought patterns, or behavior, which in turn would have led to enough trust being developed for true reconciliation, true "oneness" in heart and mind, to eventually occur.

Forgiveness is always the responsibility of the one who was offended, as Jesus said "Forgive and you will be forgiven. But if you don't forgive, you will not be forgiven." Repentance is up to the offender. Rather than turning to one's parents or children for emotional intimacy or support, a hurt spouse needs to turn to her or his spouse, holding them accountable for change,

and giving them a chance to build a new track record, perhaps through Christ-centered fellowship and accountability,
so that the two will truly become one with each other, rather
than becoming one with a parent, child, or friend. By doing
so, you will be a victor rather than a victim. Without doing so,
you will never have the marriage God wants you to have, one
through which pain leads to gain and trials turn to triumph as
each spouse empowers the other, even in "tough" ways, to
become all that God created him or her to be. This is impossible without putting Christ first, for it is He who said "They
are no longer two but one. Therefore, what God has joined
together, let nobody separate" (Matthew 19:6). Without God, a
bad marriage becomes worse. With God, a hopeless marriage
becomes hopeful, as with God all things are possible (Matthew
19:26). The best thing a mother can do for her children is to
love their father. The best thing a father can do for his children
is to love their mother. What better way to love a spouse than
how God loves us, with a love that is not excusing but forgiving, not enabling but empowering for change and growth. Let
us love one another as Christ has loved us (John 15:12). By doing so, our priorities will be right and our God will be glorified
in us and through us.

MARRIAGE MATTERS - SACRIFICIAL SUBMISSION

"Submit to one another out of reverence for Christ."

Ephesians 5:21

A Devotional based on Ephesians 5:21-33

Submission: One word filled with many negative connotations and preconceived notions in our society. It's true that God's Word exhorts wives to submit to their husbands (Ephesians 5:22). It's also true that God's Word commands husbands to love their wives (Ephesians 5:25). Wives, don't think your husbands have the easier role! Husbands, don't think your wives are your servants! Why not? In light of Genesis 1:27, 2:18-25, and the rest of God's Word, we know that the two are equally significant but perhaps not "equal," as they are not the "same," nor would God want them to be. If that were what God intended, He would have created humanity with only one gender and some other creative way of reproducing itself. Instead, we have two. At the same time, we must realize that God's design for marriage is not the "dictator-doormat" model, whether the husband is the dictator or the wife. Neither is it "Laisser-faire," where anything goes. Finally, it is not a democracy and definitely not a "partnership," where each spouse keeps track of how many contributions the other spouse makes in order to ensure that everything is tallied up in a way that is fair and equitable, without one party shorting the other when it comes to roles and responsibilities.

A husband is called to love his wife. How? As Christ loved the church (Ephesians 5:25). In other words, a husband is called to die. To what does he die? He dies to himself, even his own rights, for the sake of his wife's needs. And what does she need? She needs to be encouraged, built up, led in a way that is motivated by a husband's servant heart, leading her not so much for his sake as for hers, in order for her to one day be presented to God as radiant, without stain or blemish, holy and blameless, in her thoughts, words, and actions, as the church, Christ's bride, will one day be presented to her groom, Christ Jesus Himself (Ephesians 5:27). In other words, a husband can only be a true leader to his wife if he is a true servant to God. As a Servant Leader, he leads his wife through his self-sacrificing love, dying to his selfish ways, in order to lead in God's selfless ways, loving his wife enough to tell her what she needs to hear, whether or not it's what she wants to hear, but doing so in a firm but gentle manner, "…speaking the truth in love" (Ephesians 4:15). When you husbands die, God will not ask you how successful you were in your careers or in your churches, He'll ask you if your wife is more beautiful today than she was when He gave her to you.

A wife will joyfully submit to her husband's leadership if he consistently solicits her thoughts and feelings and concerns, her insight and wisdom on any and every issue, truly listening and valuing her input, and truly being influenced by it, before making a decision that would affect the two of them and their family. This is impossible without a husband first submitting to Christ. And if a husband first submits to Christ, he will even be submissive to his wife in a sense. But how? And what is submission anyway?

Submission is putting aside our rights for the sake of another's needs. That's what Jesus did when He put aside His right to be held in high honor as the creator of all things (Colossians 1:16) and the master of the universe (Philippians 2:10-11), being instead disrespected and tossed aside (Isaiah 53). He put aside His rights for the sake of our needs, namely, our needs of forgiveness (Romans 3:23), salvation (Romans 6:23), and guidance in this life and the next (Hebrews 10:19-25). That's true submission. And that's what God requires of all of us.

MARRIAGE MATTERS - THE ULTIMATE MARRIAGE

"For this reason a man will leave his father and mother and be united to his wife, and they will become one flesh."

Genesis 2:24

A Devotional based on Genesis 2:18-25

Single, widowed, divorced or married, God's Word has a lot to teach us in regard to relationships. In marital counseling, it is often discovered that the root issue of many problems husbands and wives face is the fact that they have never truly learned how to leave, cleave, and become one.

We are called to leave our parents not only physically, but also financially. We are called to leave them not only emotionally, but also spiritually. We are even called to leave them behaviorally! What do I mean by that? I can share an illustration from my own marriage. I was brought up in a devout Roman Catholic family of twelve children. After going to mass, our large "Sunday dinners" were often characterized by at least five conversations taking place simultaneously at the dinner table(s). My wife was brought up in a much more reserved Presbyterian family of three children. They actually waited until one person finished speaking before the next one began! Cultural differences? Yes. I grew up in the "north," and she in the "south." My family was expressive and hers reflective.

115

Behavioral differences? Absolutely. She learned to wait her turn, whereas I learned to fight for mine.

A few years into my marriage, I finally realized the part of my parents I still had not yet been able to leave. It all happened with the help of my wife, one who was determined to be a godly "helper" in the Genesis 2:20 sense, helping me become the man, husband, and father God created me to be, just as God is our "helper" (Psalm 33:20), certainly not "less" but with whom we can become "more." Most of our challenges were due to the fact that I would speak to my wife while she was trying to speak to me. The challenge continues! Yet, with the help of my wife and some godly, trusted accountability/prayer partners, I am leaving my former family, behaviorally, more and more each day in order to be a blessing to the current one.

As a result, we have cleaved and become one not only in body, but also in mind and in spirit. The beauty of a Christ-centered relationship is that we can learn to appreciate each other's differences rather than to be threatened or annoyed by them. We also can learn to complement rather than compete with each other. Lastly, we can identify what we must "leave" in order to truly cleave. As the apostle Paul eloquently explained, such a marriage often requires nothing less than death-death to ourselves as Christ died for us (Ephesians 5:25).

What if you are not currently married? Why does any of this matter? It matters to single, divorced, or widowed people just as much as it does to those of us currently married because it is all impossible without "becoming one" with the main spouse of all, Christ Jesus Himself. The church is the bride of Christ. Without peace in your eternal marriage, you will never have true peace in any temporal one. "This is a profound mystery-but I am talking about Christ and the church." (Ephesians 5:32).

BORN FREE?

At first glance, the lives of Jacob and Esau seem to demonstrate anything but freedom of choice or will. When we read Genesis 25:19-26, we are tempted to assume that Esau was "doomed" from the very beginning of his life, even during conception in his mother's womb. It seems as though choices were made for Esau before he could make them himself. The passage even appears to demonstrate that, regardless of the choices Esau would make in his life, a path was already carved out for him (see vs. 23).

King David once proclaimed to the Lord that "...My frame was not hidden from you when I was made in the secret place. When I was woven together in the depths of the earth, your eyes saw my unformed body. All the days ordained for me were written in your book before one of them came to be (Psalm 139:15, 16)." David recognized God's sovereignty. He realized his own state. He responded to God's power. He requested God's grace (vv. 23, 24).

As a result of the above, David may have sometimes felt *contained* (vv. 7-12), but usually wound up feeling *comforted* (vv. 17-18). Perhaps his response lends us something to consider in regard to the question of free-will, and how much of our *will* is actually *free*, versus the concept that when God wills the *ends*, He also wills the *means*?

We ask, what do we truly have a "say" in? What decisions can we make that will determine our future? What steps can we take in order to impact where we go? What choices do we have when we know that "In his heart a man plans his course, but the Lord determines his steps (Proverbs 16:9)?" Should we simply sit back, relax, and let God "do His thing" while we "wait and see" what He has planned for us?

I would suggest that the answer is an emphatic NO. Why? Because we *do* have a choice. We *do* have a decision to make. And we *can* have an impact on our future. We can have a "say" in what becomes of our lives through the way in which we respond to God's will for our lives.

Look again at God's plan for Jacob and Esau. The Lord's plan included the older son serving the younger one (Genesis 25:23). This was not necessarily a bad thing. It did demonstrate, however, that God does what He wants, out of His love for us, regardless of whether or not it conforms to what we want. History tells us that the ancient law of primogeniture provided that, under ordinary circumstances, the younger of two sons would be subservient to the older. God's "election" of the older son emphasizes the fact that God's people are the product not of worldly development but of His sovereign intervention in the affairs of humanity. And when He intervenes, He does so not in any arbitrary way (see Romans 9:10-14), but according to His own perfect will. Yes, much of this is a mystery. No, this does not mean you have no choices to make, as I believe the choice is in our *response*.

Esau could have responded to his life situation with humility and praise, but instead chose to respond with pride and self-centeredness. That was his choice, and that is the choice that we have. Esau's response had consequences (see Genesis 25:27-27:45), and so do ours. How will you respond to God's plan for your life?

THE ESAU TRAGEDY

What type of sorrow do you have?

Jacob may mean "deceiver," according to Hebrew scholars, but Esau allowed himself to be deceived. For a single meal, Esau sold his birthright to Jacob (Genesis 25:29-34; Hebrews 12:15-17). Was Esau sorry that he did so? Evidently not, until it was *too late*.

When Esau asked "What good is the birthright to me? (Gen. 25:32b)," he probably was not *thinking* before *speaking*. Esau perhaps put the desire of his flesh (his physical hunger) above the desire of his soul (his spiritual well-being), as at the heart of the birthright were the covenant promises that his father, Isaac, had inherited from his grandfather, Abraham, through faith in God. In such a way, Esau was said to have "despised his birthright (Gen. 25:34b)."

Esau got his meal. But he also got something else: bitterness, misery, and sorrow (Genesis 27:34-38). So much so that Esau "held a grudge against Jacob because of the blessing his father had given him. He said to himself, 'The days of mourning for my father are near; then I will kill my brother Jacob (Gen. 27:41)."

The writer of Hebrews exhorted the believers to "See to it that no one misses the grace of God and that no *bitter* root grows up to cause trouble and defile many (Hebrews 12:15, italics added)." Esau was *bitter* and his bitterness defiled many.

Why? Because he missed the boat completely! He missed the "grace of God," to which the writer of Hebrews adds: "See that no one is sexually immoral or is *godless* like Esau, who for a single meal sold his inheritance rights as the oldest son (Hebrews 12:16, italics added)." How awful to be used as an example of foolishness, around the year A.D. 70, when your "big mistake," according to historical evidence, took place around the year 1930 B.C.! Two thousand years after Esau decided to feed the flesh rather than nourish the soul, people were still talking about it, and learning from his mistakes! We are called to do the same.

What type of legacy does Esau leave us? It is a legacy of misery, brought on by a decision of tragedy, covered in tears of sorrow, as Esau "wept aloud" (Genesis 27:38b;Hebrews 12:17b) with tears of regret. But what did he regret? God's Word tells us that he wasn't sorry about choosing a meal over an everlasting feast. Rather, he was sorry that he had to pay the consequences of a foolish decision. Our actions have consequences, as Romans chapter 1 clearly demonstrates.

In 2 Corinthians 7:10, the Apostle Paul explains that "Godly sorrow brings repentance that leads to salvation and leaves no regret, but worldly sorrow brings death." Godly sorrow produced earnestness, concern, and readiness to see justice done in the Corinthians who were sorry about the right things. Rather than being sorry that they were "caught" doing something wrong (i.e. allowing a sexually immoral brother to call himself a Christ-follower but to live as anything but), they were sorry that they "did" something wrong. In other words, they were not sorry that they were "caught," but that they had sinned.

What type of sorrow do you have? When reflecting upon your sins, those things that keep you from living a life of purity, peace, and passion for Christ, separating you from the God who wants to be reconciled to you, distancing you from the God who wants you near, do you have a desire for repentance, change, that would help you rise above those things that hold you below? On the other hand, are you sorrier about being seen as a sinner than you are about your sin? Like Esau, are you more concerned about what you lose as a result of your sin than you are about the sin itself? If so, then it is time for repentance, empowered by the God who calls us to confess our sins in order for Him to forgive our sins and cleanse us from all unrighteousness (1 John 1:8, 9). Going forward, if we lack wisdom, let us ask for it from the God who gives it generously to all who ask (James 1:5). In such a way, our thoughts will produce decisions that will lead not to death but to life, as Christ is the author of life (John 15:5)!

ORDINARY PEOPLE

A Devotional based on Genesis 26:1-33

It has been said that God does *extraordinary* things through *ordinary* people. This was certainly the case with Abraham and his offspring. But why did God choose Abraham and his descendants through whom "all nations on earth will be blessed" (Gen. 22:18a)? Perhaps because Abraham *trusted* God (Gen. 15:6) and *obeyed* him (Gen. 22:18b). When Abraham first trusted, or believed, God, we read that it was "credited to him as righteousness" (Gen. 15:6). In other words, Abraham's example shows us that God graciously responds to a person's faith by crediting *righteousness* to him (see Hebrews 11:7). This is why, in the New Testament, the apostle Paul refers to Abraham as the "father of all who believe" (Romans 4:11). Genesis 15:6 is the first specific reference to faith in God's promises!

Yet, Abraham not only trusted, or had "faith in" God, but also *obeyed* Him. What reason did God give Abraham in regard to the covenant made with him? God said that He would bless Abraham and make his descendants as numerous as the stars in the sky and as the sand on the seashore, that they would take possession of the cities of their enemies, and that through them all nations on earth would be blessed, "because you have *obeyed* me" (Gen. 22:18b).

To obey is better than sacrifice (1 Samuel 15:22). And it is *obedience*, not simply "knowledge," that denotes maturity in Christ (see Matt. 7:24, 28:20, Luke 11:28, John 14:15, 23, 15:10, Acts 5:29, 32, Romans 2:13, 16:26, Heb. 5:9, James 1:22, 1 Peter 4:17, 1 John 3:24, 5:3, Revelation 12:17, 14:12, etc.)! A Christian who knows all 66 books of the Bible, memorizing many verses, yet only obeying what is convenient, is much less mature than a Christian who only knows one book of the Bible, yet obeys it consistently! I speak this way not to condemn but to convict all of us on the need to examine our hearts before the Lord, ensuring that what we know in our minds connects with how we feel in our hearts and what we do with our hands. Of course we need to always be learning God's Word in order to know what to obey. Yet, in God's eyes, as well as in the eyes of many who are watching His children carefully, actions speak louder than words. For it is what we *do* that demonstrates what we believe (James 1:22).

So what was it that Isaac and Rebekah were being asked to *trust* and *obey*? Perhaps, like their father Abraham, they were being asked to trust that God would be with them, whether in comfortable situations or costly ones, whether in plenty or in want, whether in peace or in anxiety. God perhaps wanted them to know that they could "do all things through Him who gives me strength" (Philippians 4:13). As the apostle Paul found out hundreds of years later, God desires for us to be content, regardless of what we face, knowing that He is with us. As he tells Isaac "I will be with you" (Gen. 26:3), "Do not be afraid, for I am with you..." (Gen. 26:24), so he told Abraham, and many others, that He is the God who is "with us," He is Emmanuel (see, e.g., Gen. 17:7, 26:24, 28:15, 31:3; Jos 1:5; Isa 41:10; Jer 1:8,19; Mt 28:20; Ac 18:10), the One who promises to be the sustainer and protector of His people forever. The Emmanuel theme is seen throughout the Old and New Testaments, but it is fulfilled only in the New, as it is fulfilled in Christ Jesus (Isaiah 7:14, 8:8; Matthew 1:23), as we sing "O Come O come Emmanuel."

Is Emmanuel, the God with us, with you? If not, why not? Paul tells us how we can allow Him into our lives (Romans 10:9-13), as not only the One we trust, but also the One we obey. When we trust in Jesus, God is our Savior. When we obey Jesus, God is our Lord. Jesus is not Lord at all unless He is Lord of all. Who is He in your life?

DEADLY DYSFUNCTION

A Devotional based on Genesis 26:34-28:9

My wife and I once embarked upon a contemporary phenomenon in our culture: "Creative Memories." In the midst of an often too busy life-style, we took as many photographs as we could of our daughters whom we love deeply. The pictures were then placed in photo-albums that tended to be much more creative than the run-of-the-mill, "Daddy's boast book" of photographs that I'd carry with me in my pocket. The albums tended to tell a story without speaking any words, although words may sometimes be written, or painted, onto the album. The goal was to capture the moment so as to look back upon it with grateful hearts some day long after that moment. The challenge, I believe, was to not miss out on the blessings of the moment due to being more concerned with "capturing it" than retaining it. Nevertheless, the old saying, "A picture paints a thousand words," held true.

In this Scripture passage, we are given words without a picture, and yet a portrait is indeed painted. But what kind of portrait is it? It is a family portrait. And what type of family is it? It is a highly dysfunctional one.

Upon first reading this passage, I would imagine that it is hard for many of us to *not* feel "bad" for Esau and "mad" at Jacob. Things just don't seem fair. Or do they?

Our passage shows the fulfillment of what we read in Genesis 25:19-26: God's choice of the younger son, Jacob, rather than the older son, Esau, as the recipient of His promises to Abraham and Isaac (see Gen. 17:4-8, 19-22; 22:15-18; 26:2-5). In choosing the younger son rather than the older one, God overrules the natural with the supernatural, putting aside the ancient law of primogeniture which provided the younger son as a servant to the older, and instead reversing the traditional order and the will of man with a new order infused by the will of God. Esau becomes Jacob's servant.

If God is sovereign, then His will *will* be done. If God is in control, then our lives need not be out of control. If we trust in God, then we need not rely solely on others. If we have faith in God, then we need not lose faith in our future. Yet, in our passage, we see a family that unfortunately did not apply these truths to their lives. Although Rebekah had been told that God would bless Jacob (Gen. 25:23), she felt she had to "help God" along (27:5-17) through disguising the truth and deceiving her husband. Perhaps she felt "the end justifies the means," as her means were anything but just. She accomplished a plan that was good by travelling down a path that was bad.

Consider this family. Jacob blatantly lies over and over again in order to receive the blessing that was his anyway (27:19, 20, 24, etc.). He chose to gain something good by doing something bad. Esau, on the other hand, already knew that he had been deceived out of his birthright (27:36), which would be fulfilled in his blessing. Yet, he chooses unforgiveness and revenge for the lack of justice as a means to accomplishing what he felt was just, rather than leaving justice in God's hands (27:41), letting God be the judge. Rebekah often manipulates

Isaac through Jacob and Jacob through Isaac (27:5-17, 27:46) to get what she wants, rather than communicating directly to Isaac in order to experience what she needs. Isaac, who allows all of this to take place in his family, takes "favorites" as he refers to Esau as *my* son (27:1), enabling Rebekah to do the same with Jacob (27:13).

Isaac's family was anything but perfect. Likewise, our families are anything but perfect. Yet, we can become more like the One who is perfect if we do things His way, rather than our way, surrendering our will to His, and inviting Him to be the ruler of our lives (John 15:5).

How well are you doing at treating others the way that you would like them to treat you (Matt. 7:12)? When another person offends you, how well are you at talking *to* them rather than talking *about* them, to resolve the conflict? (Matthew 7:1-6, 18:15-20)? Where there's a will there's a way, and with God all things are possible. When fulfilling what is revealed as God's plan for our lives, we can either rely upon our *natural* human tendencies or on God's *supernatural* empowerment We can rely on ourselves, or rely on the Spirit, gratifying our own sinful nature, or living by God's own liberating Spirit (Galatians 5:16-26). If we walk in the Spirit, exercising patience and self-control, among other fruit, as we cry out to God, we will find life and live it abundantly (John 10:10). If not, we may feel otherwise.

Jacob had blatantly lied over and over again in order to receive his father's blessing, so that his brother Esau would not (27:19, 20, 24, etc.). He chose to gain something good by doing something bad. He failed to treat others as he would have them treat him (Matthew 7:12). As a result of his lack of character and integrity, he suffered, as did Leah and Rachel, later on in his life. Jacob, the example of what happens when we walk in the "flesh," putting our needs above the needs of others, shows us that when we do so, we will find death, and die in despair (Romans 6:23). Which will you choose?

WHAT GOES AROUND COMES AROUND

A Devotional based on Genesis 29:1-30

After reading Genesis 26:34 through 27:45, it would be difficult for many of us to *not* feel "bad" for Esau and "mad" at Jacob. The statement was made that "Things just don't seem fair." The "deceiver," was deceived, and was surprised about something that should not have surprised him. Jacob, who played many tricks on others, was amazed that Laban would play a trick on him (29:25).

We often say we believe in treating others the way that we would want them to treat us, but do we resolve to live what we say we believe, or do we simply make such statements with selfish motives or hidden agendas? If we answer "yes" to the latter rather than the former, we deceive ourselves, as we soon will learn that we are called to treat others as we would want them to treat us, not only for their own good, but for ours.

God's Word tells us, "If someone says, 'I love God,' and yet hates his brother, he is a liar; for the one who does not love his brother whom he has seen, cannot love God whom he has not seen (1 John 4:20)." How well are you at loving your "brother" or "sister?" How are you doing in treating others the way that you would like them to treat you (Matt. 7:12)? When you have particular wishes and desires, do you value your desires more than the people affected by those desires? Are you "looking out for # 1," or placing the needs of others above your own needs (Philippians 2:5-11)? If we belong to God, we will love one another unselfishly, "...for love is from God; and every one who loves is born of God and knows God. The one who does not love does not know God, for God is love (1 John 4:7, 8)." If we follow God's ways, we will live abundantly. On the other hand, if we walk in our selfish ways, putting our needs above the needs of others, we will find death, and die in despair (Romans 6:23).

God is a God of justice. Yet, although He is also a God of mercy, His creation are often children of judgment. Therefore, obeying God protects us from evil. In a selfish world, we have a choice to either love things and use others, or use things and love others. If we treat other people as a means to accomplish our own ends, we will have to answer to Christ in the very end (Romans 14:10). Yet, if we treat others as we would want them to treat us, then we won't be afraid of the truth that "what goes around comes around" and we will hear our Lord one day say, "Well done, good and faithful servant." What will you choose?

NOT YOUR WILL BUT MINE BE DONE?

A Devotional based on Genesis 29:31-30:43

There are some good characteristics that Jacob, Rachel, Leah, and Laban displayed. At the same time, there are some "not so good" qualities. Even though Leah became Jacob's first wife, she was not the "beloved" wife. She was painfully aware of this situation. In fact, even the birth of four sons could not comfort her. She longed for the affection of Jacob, and made her longing public by naming her first son Reuben, meaning "See, a son," whom the 'Lord had given her' as He saw her misery and consoled her with a son. She named the second one "Simeone," meaning "He hears," implying that the Lord had heard that her husband didn't love her. Her third she named "Levi," "attached," meaning that she hoped that this son would help Jacob become more attached to her than to Rachel. Finally, "Judah," "praise," meant that she wanted to do nothing but praise the Lord. Yet, Jacob still paid no attention to her. Rachel, on the other hand, who had Jacob's attention, could bear no children to him for quite a while. Rather than wait on the Lord in faith and trust, Rachel threw her maid upon Jacob. Like Sarah and Rebekah, Rachel too was childless. Yet, unlike Sarah and Rebekah, Rachel did not have the maturity of faith to accept God's will and plan for her in blessing her with children in His timing. This may have been very difficult for Rachel, as it may be for most of us, especially when others around us are having no problem at all conceiving and giving birth to children. It requires trust that God knows what's best for us, even when we cannot understand it ourselves (Proverbs 3:5, 6; Romans 8:28, 29).

Rachel manipulated Leah for mandrake plants (30:14), thought to induce fertility. Instead of turning to the One and only true God, she turned to a false one. By handing these plants over to Rachel, Leah in essence "hired" Rachel's husband that night, and became the mother of Issachar, whose name is a play on the Hebrew for "hire."

This far from ideal story of the pitfalls and disasters of polygamy goes on and on. Even Jacob, whose wives continue getting "one up" on each other, tries to do the same to Laban, who he believes is deceiving him regarding his wages for the work he has done over the years on Laban's land. Even though Jacob may have talked about what God had done for him, he continued in his "opportunism," being just as manipulative of an individual as he was twenty years earlier.

We all have a little bit of Jacob, Laban, Rachel, and Leah in us. We all have a little bit of "restlessness" when it comes to waiting on the Lord for His blessings in our lives. But what can we do about it? Sin is destructive, and anything that separates us from God's type of love (1 Corinthians 13) is sin. When we seek God's will for our lives, everything else falls into its proper place (Matthew 6:33). Yet, if we follow our own selfish ways, everything falls apart.

Jesus said, "Come to me, all you who are weary and burdened, and I will give you rest." If we turn to Him, instead of our own devices, perhaps we will truly experience the rest and peace we are promised by our faith in Christ. If not, we may be wearily pursuing our own interests at everyone else's expense, and damaging ourselves in the process.

PURSUING THE WILL OF GOD

A Devotional based on Genesis 31:1-32:2

How can you know the will of God? How can we know where He is leading us in our lives? How do we know for sure that we are taking the right steps to head down the right path in order to accomplish the right things during our time on this earth? These questions have no easy answers, nor have they ever. However, thankfully, as believers in Jesus Christ we are given the guidance of the Holy Spirit (John 14) who empowers us to understand the counsel of God's Word (Psalm 1) in navigating through the stages of our lives. After all, the Bible tells us that "All Scripture is God-breathed and is useful for teaching, rebuking, correcting and training in righteousness, so that the person of God may be thoroughly equipped for every good work (2 Timothy 3:16,17)."

But what do we do when the leading of God is not so clear in our particular lives? How do we know what to do next when our decisions often seem arbitrary or overly subjective? When do we know for sure that we are in the "center of God's will" regarding who we marry (if we do not remain single), where we work, where we live, and how we respond to various circumstances in our lives that are beyond our control?

Jacob might have asked the same types of questions. The Word of the Lord clearly told him to "Go back to the land of your fathers and to your relatives (Gen. 31:3)." So what did

Jacob do? He *obeyed* God and left the home of Laban, his father-in-law, with whom he was at odds. If Jacob waited until Laban was happy with his decision, he may never have left! If Jacob waited until he and others affected by his move had a "peace" about his departure, he could have become more concerned with pleasing man rather than pleasing God. Yet, sometimes we today, even as Christ-followers, give in to the cultural misconception that we need to have a "peace" about something before we act upon whatever that "something" is. We take the Apostle Paul's words to us written in Philippians 4:6-7 out of context. As a result, we miss the boat in following God's will for our lives.

My wife and I had a difficult decision to make back in 1995. We were living in Boston, our "favorite" city. We had both been recently promoted in our careers in the financial services industry. We loved our church family with all of our hearts. We loved the neighborhood within which we lived. We were grateful to be living close, but not "too close," to family members. We were "D.I.N.K.s" (Double Income No Kids) who felt free to go wherever the Lord led us. This seemed to be a good thing, until He opened up the possibility for us to go to California where I would attend seminary in preparation for vocational ministry.

Sending us to California was similar to sending Jonah to Ninevah-it was the last place we would have wanted to go. Yet, with the right circumstances, the godly counsel of older, wiser believers, knowing that nothing we were doing was in opposition to God's Word regarding trusting Him and loving others, we prayerfully took a "step of faith." In an old vehicle, we drove 3,300 miles away without a place to live and without a job, having just enough funds for tuition and a hotel room. There were many unanswered questions. Most of all, we had no "peace" about it all. So why did we go? We trusted that we were following God's will because we prayed for His intervention (Proverbs 3:5, 6), we sought the counsel of older, wiser Christians, and we considered the calling to prepare for a change in vocation. We were united about the decision, remembering that the Spirit brings unity among believers on many such decisions, provided the believers are seeking God's will and not their own, requiring us to do nothing illegal, immoral, or sinful (i.e. Acts 15:28). As a result, we went.

Thankfully, Jacob didn't wait for everybody to *approve* of his decisions. He sought God's will, responded to the command of the Lord with obedience, and moved on. We too, perhaps on a much smaller scale, sought the right leading in the right way, and moved on. In retrospect we are very glad we did. Our "Ninevah" turned out to be a place of deliverance for us and many others. As we ministered to Californians, they ministered to us. God showed us our weaknesses and strengthened us for the days ahead. The "days ahead" included a place in which we could have never even imagined while in California. In a sense, the Lord sent me back to my "homeland" of New England, as he sent Jacob back to his homeland. God may send you away from home, never to return, until you join Him in our heavenly home. Either way, if we surrender our wills to His will, knowing that we may not always go where we want to go, but where we need to go, He can continue His work in our lives with many unexpected blessings along the way. To God be the glory!

WHEN FAITH MEANS MORE THAN FAMILY, FRIENDS, AND FORTUNE

A Devotional based on Genesis 32:1-32

Jacob, like many of us, was faced with a dilemma: Leaving behind a bad situation with his father-in-law, he went ahead to a bad situation with his brother, Esau, with whom he had been at odds. He naturally became concerned about Esau's response to him-and perhaps even wondered if Esau was still harboring any bitterness towards him due to the way in which Jacob had treated him in the past. He learned, through sending messengers ahead of himself, that Esau, along with 400 men, was on his way to meet him.

How would you feel if you were in Jacob's place? How would you be affected by the type of news he received, given the circumstances? How should Jacob respond?

Jacob responded in many ways. Emotionally, he was filled with "fear and distress (vs. 7)." Mentally, he made decisions to divide his people and his possessions into two groups, "spreading the wealth," hoping that at least one of these diversified investments would survive (vs. 8). Next, Jacob cried out to God for help and protection (vv. 9-12), reminding God of His promise to allow Jacob to have prosperity in his lifetime. Then Jacob prepared a gift for Esau, instructing his servants to let

Esau know as soon as possible that his brother wants to shower him with gifts. His motive? "...he (Jacob) thought, 'I will pacify him (Esau) with these gifts I'm sending on ahead; later, when I see him, perhaps he will receive me (vs. 20)." What else was Jacob thinking? Perhaps Jacob was thinking that he could buy his brother's forgiveness, and God's protection.

How often, when we are frightened, do we first turn to means of self-delivery rather than to the Deliverer Himself? It was good that Jacob prayed after he reacted. It would have been even better if he prayed *before* he reacted. Why? Because so often we have what Christian counselors and theologians would call a "fear of man" (i.e. Esau) problem, before we even realize that we *need* a fear of God factor. Only then will we have the right perspective in our troubles. As Jesus said to his disciples in a word of encouragement (and exhortation), "Do not be afraid of those who kill the body but cannot kill the soul. Rather, be afraid of the One who can destroy both soul and body in hell (Matthew 10:28)." These are tough words to take outside of the context within which they were written, the context of Jesus' reminder that when we turn to Him, we need not fear anything, as He is more powerful than everything. Thankfully, for those who call out to him (Romans 10: 9-13), He uses that power to care for us and protect us (see Matthew 10:17-42), rather than punish us, because of His great love for us.

We read about Jacob wrestling with God (vv. 22-32). Jacob had struggled to prevail first with Esau and then with Laban. Yet, when God wrestled him, he finally realized that it was with God that he had been wrestling all along. It was God who held Jacob's destiny in His hands, as He does ours. Jacob acknowledged God as the ultimate source of blessing, loving the Blesser more than the blessings, the Gift-Giver more than the gifts. Only then could he enter the Promised Land. Yet, as a result of his wrestling, he entered with a limp, a permanent reminder of his need to rely on God and not himself, following God's lead rather than going against it.

The Apostle Paul learned the same lesson (Acts 9:1-19). Perhaps you and I have also learned, or are beginning to learn, that when we place our hands in the hand of the Lord Jesus Christ, and allow Him to lead us, we live. We begin to see, often contrary to our culture, that our significance does not come from our family, fame, or fortune, but from our faith. We do not rely on our peace, privacy, and prosperity, but God's power, for protection, and promise of hope, in this world and the world to come.

In the words of a song popular several decades ago, "Put your hands in the Hand of the Man who stilled the water...Put your hand in the Hand of the Man who calmed the sea...Take a look at yourself, and you will look at others differently...Put your hands in the Hand of the Man from Galilee."

Who is holding your hand? In what are you being led? Will you wrestle with God or rest in Him? Jesus said, "Come to me, all you who are weary and burdened, and I will give you rest. Take my yoke upon you and learn from me, for I am gentle and humble in heart, and you will find rest for your souls. For my yoke is easy and my burden is light (Matthew 11:28-30). May that truth be realized in your life!

THANKSGIVING: SOMETHING FOR WHICH TO BE THANKFUL

"Do not repay anyone evil for evil. Be careful to do what is right in the eyes of everybody. If it is possible, as far as it depends on you, live at peace with everyone. Do not take revenge, my friends, but leave room for God's wrath, for it is written: 'It is mine to avenge; I will repay,' says the Lord. On the contrary: 'If your enemy is hungry, feed him; if he is thirsty, give him something to drink. In doing this, you will heap burning coals on his head.' "

Romans 12:17-21

The holidays are thought of as being a time of cheer, joy, excitement, fun, and thanksgiving. And they are for some of us. But often they are a time of bitterness, resentment, frustration, sadness, depression, and anger, especially for families scarred by hurt **and** pain.

The issue of hurt and pain is a continuous one in our society. Whether it's the hurt of having to spend another holiday season as a single mom or dad, or just as a single person, or even the pain of deciding who we'll spend Thanksgiving dinner with this Thursday-will it be our parents, our sister, our brother, our friends, mother and her new husband, father and his new wife, step-sister, step-brother, half brother on the ex-stepmother in law's side of our cousin's next door neighbor (it can get very confusing for some of us)!

Then there's the question of whom we are getting along with best right now, and who we are mad at, who we don't even want to think about during Thanksgiving or Christmas. For the ones we don't like, we may even think of hosting dinner at our home and inviting everybody but them. We can think of many creative ways by which we might "get even" with them during the holidays, how we can hurt others back for all the hurt they've caused us, or how we can make sure that Barbara or Tom doesn't get his or her way any more. Either way, the holiday season is often not the most "joyous" time for many people.

Why is this so? Perhaps because we have too many things to "take care of," to "get even for," or to make right or fair in our own way. Too many situations to rectify. The Word of God has a lot to say about these issues. Through Romans 12:17-21 (printed above), God exhorts us to not be overcome by evil, or repay evil with evil. How is this possible, when it includes the evil of hurt and pain, or the evil of selfishness, or jealousy, or anything else? Only through forgiveness.

Forgiveness is a means through which we can gain something for which we can truly be thankful each Thanksgiving and Holiday season and throughout the year. But why should we forgive? And how can we forgive?

I believe there are four steps by which we become able to forgive. First, we can consider our reasons for unforgiveness. There are many. One is that "the offense was too great." This is when we feel as though what someone has done is too great a sin to forgive. To make matters worse, we may be upset that "he or she isn't truly sorry." Even when somebody doesn't recognize the trouble they've caused us, we hold it against them and refuse to let go. The fact that they don't even realize what they've done, or at least act as if they don't, makes us resentful towards them. Another reason for unforgiveness is that "he or she did it again." Perhaps a wife gave her husband another chance of being more affectionate to her and the children, and it worked for a little while, but then, he "did it again"-and she thinks, "that is it!" And the whole conflict is set in motion again. Finally, and perhaps most dominant, is that we feel someone has to punish the person whom we are refusing to forgive for what they have done. How often do we want God to be merciful to us and yet want Him to skin other people alive? We may at first wait patiently for "God to get them," or for their schemes to backfire on them, figuring that what goes around comes around. But when we don't see them eventually suffer, we sometimes take it upon ourselves to be God's hand of vengeance. We become full of hatred and the need to get revenge. We paradoxically give power over ourselves to the person we attempt to control by not forgiving him or her. This happens when we are lacking true love in our lives, for we read in 1 Corinthians 13:5 that "…love keeps no record of wrongs." But why shouldn't we keep a record? Why wouldn't we want to keep track of the score? When we consider some of the results of unforgiveness in our very own lives, we may see why.

And that is why the second step by which we become able to forgive is that we consider the results of unforgiveness. Although there are several, I will only mention four:

"Self-inflicted reinjury"-when, every time we see the person who has hurt us, or even just think of them, or hear them, or just hear their name, we cringe, or we find ourselves becoming filled with anger again, remembering what they did to us or someone we love, such as our spouse, child, sibling, or friend. We relive all that they did to us, as well as the accompanying hurt that it caused us; "No More Love"-when someone hurt by a past significant other withdraws from potential new significant others, refusing to love anymore. Their refusal to love stems from their unforgiveness of the one they used to love; "Walls Go Up"-keeping others out of our lives, so that they cannot hurt us, we become anxious and threatened when personal intimacy becomes possible. We refuse to let others into our personal thoughts and concerns; "Bitterness"-when we think others don't notice what's going on inside, but our bitterness can usually be detected by even a casual observer. This is perhaps the most damaging consequence of the sin of unforgiveness, ignoring God's Will for us as Christ-followers. As he has told us in His Word, "See to it that no one comes short of the grace of God; that no root of bitterness springing up causes trouble, and by it many be defiled (Hebrews 12:15)." God is aware of the pain of bitterness, and other results of our unforgiveness. He loves us enough to show us the way out of it, which leads to our next step.

A third step by which we become able to forgive is when we consider receiving God's forgiveness. We recognize our need for it, admitting that we are not perfect, and are just as imperfect as those around us who have caused us grief in many ways. As we read in Romans 3:23, "...all have sinned and fall short of the glory of God." That means all of us, there are no exceptions. With this in mind, we are told by Jesus Himself through Matthew 9:13 that He did not come for the righteous but sinners.

Next, we must ask for forgiveness. The Word of God tells us that "All the prophets testify about him (Christ) that everyone who believes in him receives forgiveness of sins through his name (Acts 10:43)." No matter how "bad" the sins are. Why is this so? It's because the ultimate payment for our sins, receiving spiritual death in addition to our physical death that we all will die, was removed by Christ who died for it on the cross. It's not that God is a Santa Claus kind of God who forgives us just because we ask, but He's a righteous God who doesn't justify sin. Instead, He can't have anything to do with sin. He can't even look at it, because He is holy, perfect and righteous. He never justifies sin, saying, "Oh, don't worry about it, it's part of being human." Yet, He will justify the sinner, the person who sins, if the sinner acknowledges his or her need to be considered as righteous as Jesus, who alone walked this earth without sinning, in order to be forgiven by and reconciled to God. This is only possible when we let Jesus take our place on the cross, dying for our sinful nature, our imperfect nature, so that we may be considered as perfect as He is, in our new Spirit nature. That is our entrance ticket into God's family. That is our Thanksgiving feast. That is our Christmas present, if we accept it.

God's forgiveness is not a cheap kind of forgiveness. It was not cheap at all, as it cost God a lot. It cost Him his one and only Son, making our position perfect, although our condition is "not yet there," as we continue to be sanctified through the work of the Holy Spirit in our lives. In fulfillment of God's plan for us to be reconciled with Him and reunited to our creator, in Whose image we are created, He (God in the flesh, Jesus) was punished brutally (Isaiah 53). So if we think there's need for more punishment of all sins than that, and that we have to inflict such punishment on others, and even on ourselves, by not receiving His forgiveness and not forgiving others as we have been forgiven, then we are badly mistaken. And that leads to our final step.

The fourth step by which we become able to forgive is when we consider some of the results of God's forgiveness. The first is eternal life (Romans 6:23). A second is freedom from condemnation (Romans 8:1). When we realize how much we ourselves have been forgiven, how much has been completely wiped off the records by Christ's blood, that our sinful thoughts, words, and actions of the past, present, and future will never be held against us as they've been held against Christ on our behalf, we become truly able to forgive others. This exchange changes our very nature, as the Word tells us, "God made him who had no sin to be sin for us, so that in him we might become the righteousness of God (2 Cor. 5:21)." How amazing to think that we not only have a change in our position before God, but also growth in our condition on this earth, so that we can live a life of abundant contentment, fulfilled by the things that God designed for us to be fulfilled-the things that last eternally-the gifts that are inward and not outward (Galatians 5:22,23). So we are free to simply live our life for Him in all we do, bringing glory to Him, and looking forward to our Heavenly home with Him, in a place of no bitterness, resentment, anger, frustration, hurt, or any other sins that keep us from becoming all that we were created to be.

I believe that our ability to forgive others is directly proportionate to the extent to which we have received God's forgiveness-in every area of our lives. The degree to which you will be able to love and forgive others is dependent upon your acceptance of God's love for you and His forgiveness for your sins. Will you accept that forgiveness? If so, you will truly have something for which to be thankful this Thanksgiving and always.

WHAT'S THE BIG DEAL ABOUT THE RESSURRECTION?

"And if Christ has not been raised, our preaching is useless and so is your faith."

1 Corinthians 15:14

Jesus never asked His disciples to remember His birth. But He did instruct them to remember His death and resurrection. "For every time you eat this bread and drink this cup, you are announcing the Lord's death until He comes again (1 Corinthians 11:26)." When we reflect upon the Last Supper, the crucifixion, and the resurrection of Jesus, we are called to do at least two things: First, look back at Jesus' atoning death on the cross. Second, look forward to Jesus' second coming. Without the shedding of blood, there would be no forgiveness of sins (Hebrews 9:22). And without the resurrection, our faith would be in vain (1 Corinthians 15:13)!

The Good News is that Jesus *is* risen from the dead, just as those of us who trust in Him will rise also. As we read in Scripture, "...Christ has indeed been raised from the dead, the firstfruits of those who have fallen asleep. For since death came through a man, the resurrection of the dead comes also through a man. For as in Adam all die, so in Christ all will be made alive (1 Corinthians 15:20-22)."

When we receive Christ as our Lord and Savior (John 3:16, 17) by faith, rather than works (Ephesians 2:8, 9), we are promised eternal life (Romans 6:23). Yet, it gets even better. We are not only offered *eternal* life but also an *abundant* life (John 10:10) with internal peace despite external problems. This is why the Apostle Paul stated that if anyone is in Christ he is a new creation, the old has gone and the new has come (2 Corinthians 5:17). Here's the big question: How willing are you to choose to let your new nature overcome the old?

The truth of our new nature in Christ is not that in Christ it is impossible to sin, but that in any given circumstance it is possible *not* to sin. The Bible tells us that the choice is ours. When you celebrate Easter, the day of resurrection, why not ask the Lord to empower you to rise above all that holds you below, in your thoughts, words, and actions? If we are willing to surrender, saying "not my will but Yours be done," and are willing to "take up our crosses" to follow Him, we will die to the sinful human nature identified with Adam, and live to the fulfilling spiritual nature identified with Christ. Only then can we enjoy the experience of the *empty tomb*, the resurrected life, free from everything that hinders us, both now and forever (Hebrews 12:1-3).

When you become a new creation in Christ, all of heaven celebrates (Luke 15:7), as you have passed from death into life, and you will never be condemned (John 5:24). Regardless of when you were born, you have a new "birthday" because you were born not only physically, but now spiritually, as your eyes are opened up to God's truth (John 3:3). You are off to a new beginning in your life.

Easter is the perfect time for "new beginnings," for both seekers and believers. God never forces us to follow His will for our lives over our own. He *invites* us to do so. Yet, when we follow His will through His Word and His Spirit, we experience life. When we stick to our own will, we experience death- emotionally, physically, and even spiritually. The choice is ours. Which will you choose?

WHOSE FAITH DO YOU HAVE?

"For we must all appear before the judgment seat of Christ, that each one may receive what is due him for the things done while in the body, whether good or bad."

2 Corinthians 5:10

It's been said that God has no grandchildren. Jesus paid the price of salvation for the whole world, but only those who say yes to Him will actually become *children* of God (John 1:12). Faith in Christ can not be "passed on" to the next generation as traditions might be. At least not authentically.

Even though the Bible emphasizes the fact that we must individually receive Christ and His gift of salvation, this is the most overlooked part of the message in a lot of houses of worship today. So many people are left with the impression that if they go to church, or are born into a Christian family, or try to be moral and religious, then they are automatically made right with God. But it's not true. Anyone who relies on their own efforts, or the efforts of another human being, be they one's parents, grandparents, or friends, to be accepted into God's family, is eventually going to experience the world's worst nightmare (Romans 6:23, Ephesians 2:8,9).

Each of us is invited to receive the forgiveness and leadership of Christ individually. And when we do, God's Word assures us that the Holy Spirit will immediately take residence within us and begin to change us from the inside out in order for us to become who God made us to be.

And so you have two options: You can either reject the son, and identify yourself with Adam's race, a race flawed by sin, or you can embrace the Son, and identity yourself with a race freed from sin. The consequence of the first option is that we would suffer endless punishment. As John says in John 3:36, "whoever rejects the Son will not see life, for God's wrath remains on him."

Jesus Himself, in John 3:16-18, is recorded as saying "For God so loved the world that he gave his one and only Son, that whoever believes in him will not perish but will have eternal life. For God did not send his Son into the world to condemn the world, but to save the world through him. Whoever believes in him is not condemned, but whoever does not believe stands condemned already because he has not believed in the name of God's one and only Son."

The Word of God teaches that God has no grandchildren. You have a choice to either become a child of God, and live like one, or be an orphan in the end. The choice is yours (Joshua 24:15). Which will you choose?

COMPELLING COMPASSION

What motivates us to share our faith in Jesus Christ, both locally and globally, at a time during which "religious pluralism" and "social relativism" are the norm in our society. We might also ask what was it that made Jesus' message a message of "good news" at a time when certain others viewed it as anything but good. After all, the belief that there were many roads that led to God, and that all truth is relative, was "alive and well" during the first century AD (i.e. John 4:19-24, John 18:38). This is what made Jesus' message, "I am the way, the *truth*, and the life... (John 14:6)," so counter-cultural. Scripture tells us over and over again that Jesus is the One and Only way to eternal life (Romans 6:23).

What difference does this make? All the difference in the world. Without Jesus, we are like sheep without a shepherd, harassed and helpless, seeing and yet blind, hearing and yet deaf, misleading and misled, wandering aimlessly through life with no true meaning, purpose, or direction. What a sad predicament. This is why Jesus had *compassion* on the crowds (Matthew 9:36). He knew that regardless of what they *thought* was the way, He *knew* what the way was. *He* is the way, and it is a way that leads to not only an abundant life (John 10:10) but an eternal one (John 3:16).

Jesus could have told the crowds what many people wanted to hear. He could have told them that they could create their own god, putting God in a box, making Him out to be the kind of god that they could accept, a god who is "inclusive," not only of people, but of all of their desires and ideologies, whether good or bad. He could have allowed them to believe in a god who lets them "call the shots" on who's "in" and who's "out" when it came to heaven. He could have told them and us what our itching ears *want* to hear (2 Timothy 4:3, 4 ff.), rather than what we *need* to hear. But He loved them, and us, too much to do so. He could not lie, because He not only knows the truth but He *is* the truth (John 18:37).

Although God is not "inclusive" of all kinds of faith, He is inclusive of the faith of all kinds of people, as long as their faith is placed in Him (Galatians 3:26-29). Why? Because *lost people matter to God.* He does not want "anyone to perish, but everyone to come to repentance (2 Peter 3:9)." And that is why we are called not to coerce others into faith in Christ, but to pray for them to come to a saving knowledge of Jesus Christ. If we are motivated by compassion for others, as Jesus had compassion upon us, we will pray for them, first talking to God about them before talking to them about God. "This is good and pleases God our Savior, who wants everyone to be saved and to come to a knowledge of the truth. For there is one God and one mediator between God and man, the man Christ Jesus… (1 Timothy 2:3-5)."

What keeps you from sharing your faith with others? What motivates you to share it? Are you more concerned with proving yourself "right" and others "wrong" when it comes to objective truth, or are you more concerned for the emotional, psychological, and spiritual well-being of God's lost sheep who have not yet been found? If we allow Jesus' love for us to motivate us to share His love with others, we will truly make the invisible Christ visible, bringing healing to those who are hurt, hope to the hopeless, peace to the anxious, sight to the blind, and direction to the lost. What greater purpose could there possibly be for our lives?

PURPOSEFUL PASSION

When it comes to bringing the Good News of Jesus Christ to those who have been plagued with the "bad news" of this world, sending and suffering often go together. We are called to become People of Purpose. Yet often in fulfilling our purpose as Christ-followers (Matthew 28:19, 20), we are asked to endure *passion*, suffering, for Christ. That suffering can be as small as the mockery of a loved one who ridicules our faith in Jesus, falsely accusing us of committing "intellectual suicide," or worse yet, falsely accusing us of being "narrow-minded bigots filled with hatred towards others." As Jesus said, "If the head of the house has been called Beelzebub, how much more the members of his household?" (Matthew 10:25). The suffering could also include intense persecution, even to the point of shedding blood, being *martyred*, because we refuse to recant our faith in Jesus Christ, as many believers before us have been asked to do. Yet Jesus shared that "Whoever finds his life will lose it, and whoever loses his life for my sake will find it." (Matthew 10:39). In a similar way, Jesus also had said, "Whoever acknowledges me before others, I will also acknowledge before my Father in heaven. But whoever disowns me before others, I will also disown before my Father in heaven." (Matthew 10:32).

How could Jesus share such "harsh" challenges? Let me share one thought. But first, allow me to share an illustration. On a wall of my office hangs an oil on canvas painting of

155

"The Hope Café" by David Maier, a local artist. It has seldom gone unnoticed by guests in my office, particularly those feeling "down and out," "left out" or "rejected" by God. The portrait displays just the opposite message to them regarding how much they matter to God.

We read in God's Word: "Now the tax collectors and 'sinners' were all gathering around to hear him. But the Pharisees and the teachers of the Law muttered, 'This man welcomes sinners and eats with them.' On hearing this, Jesus said to them, 'It is not the healthy who need a doctor, but the sick. I have not come to call the righteous, but sinners." (from Luke 15:1 and Mark 2:17).

We are all sick, and not one of us is righteous (Romans 3:23). The difference lies in whether or not we admit it. How sick are you? How unrighteous are you? In the words of the artist: "In 'The Hope Café,' we see Jesus doing what He always does. He is where his beloved children are; talking to them in terms they can understand. In life, as in this painting, everyone reacts to Jesus a little differently. In the Great Commission, we were commanded to 'go and tell.' It means to go into ALL the world. Even a seedy run down place like 'The Hope Café.'"

So why ask others if they will accept what many of them will reject? Because even in the process of persecuting the messengers of the Good News, the message of the Good News could get through to the persecutor. Even at a time when there are many negative connotations and preconceived notions of what it means to be a Christian, those who misunderstand may be made to understand. After all, look at what happened to the Apostle Paul, who admits having persecuted the church, even to death (see Acts 8:3, Philippians 3, etc.). His life was so changed by the love of Christ which was in the messengers of Christ, that he was prepared to accept the message of Christ, after seeing it "fleshed out" through His followers. If we are to know Christ and make Him known, then we must refuse to separate ourselves from the world. Instead, we must be *in* the world but not *of* it, practicing what we preach, walking what we talk, "fleshing out" the Good News that can set us free. As a result, when others see us, they will see Christ, and turn to Him out of their own captivity and into His freedom, both now and forever.

AFFIRMED BY THE FATHER

Nobody ever died from receiving too much affirmation. However, some may have died from a lack thereof. Where do we go for affirmation? There are many choices, including parents, siblings, children, friends, coworkers, neighbors, teachers, employers, political parties, social clubs, country clubs, bars and athletic arenas. Some of us even look to church leaders. Yet, not all of these choices are healthy. Many of our choices are based upon convenience rather than cost. Take, for example, receiving affirmation from a friend. If a friend is the type of friend whose acceptance includes not only acceptance of you but also acceptance of your thoughts, words, and behavior, even if those very things are destructive and detrimental to your well being in the long run, then that friend is not a true friend.

Scripture tells us that there is a friend who sticks closer than a brother (Proverbs 18:24). That friend is Jesus Christ (John 15:13-15). It may at first seem harsh that Jesus tells us that "Anyone who loves his father or mother more than me is not worthy of me; anyone who loves his son or daughter more than me is not worthy of me... (Matthew 10:37)." Yet, when we consider the condition of our brothers, sisters, mothers, fathers, and others, we realize that human beings are capable of disappointing us, "letting us down," and even neglecting us. Just look at what happens when we offend a brother: "An offended brother is more unyielding than a fortified city... (Proverbs 18:19)." Yet, when we offended God, when we rejected His truth in acceptance of our lies, how did He respond? The Apostle Paul reminds us that "While we were still sinners, Christ died for us (Romans 5:8)."

Friendships with others often have costs, whether known or unknown. A good salesperson once told me that price, or cost, is only an issue in the absence of value. In order for God to welcome us as friends, He had to give His one and only Son (John 3:16), in order to not only be just but the one by whom we are justified (Romans 3:21-26). The cost was great. Yet, in God's eyes, the value of your friendship, your unity with Him, is even greater. You matter to God.

What about our cost? What price do we have to pay? Scripture tells us that Jesus paid the price for our sins, in order for us to be reconciled to God (Romans 6:23). He paid a debt that He did not owe because we owed a debt that we could not pay. But what does following Jesus *cost me* personally? It costs me my life. Jesus said, "Whoever finds his life will lose it, and whoever loses his life for my sake will find it (Matthew 10:39)." Will you lose your life to find and enjoy true life through Jesus, the Author of Life? I pray that you will.

CONCLUSION

Now that you have chewed on some "food for thought," I hope and pray that you will turn what you've digested into energy for doing what is right in a world that has gone wrong. My prayer for you is that you will remain in His peace in the midst of life's problems, trusting in the One who has overcome the world (John 16:33). I also pray that the Holy Spirit will help you to daily rely on The One who said "Come, all you who are thirsty, come to the waters; (Isaiah 55:1a)" for "…whoever drinks the water I give him will never thirst. Indeed, the water I give him will become in him a spring of water welling up to eternal life (John 4:14)." May you know His blessings until you see Him face to face when you drink in joy at that great banquet which He has prepared for those who love Him (Psalm 23)!

CPSIA information can be obtained
at www.ICGtesting.com
Printed in the USA
LVOW11s1958140917
548798LV00001B/18/P